BEE COUNTY COLLEGE
DATE DUE

HANDBOOK FOR TEACHER AIDES

HANDBOOK FOR TEACHER AIDES

HOWARD BRIGHTON

International Standard Book Number: 0-87812-017-3
Library of Congress Catalog Card Number: 71-168583

© 1972 by
Pendell Publishing Company
Midland, Michigan

All Rights Reserved
Published 1972
Printed in the United States of America

To Patricia for her devotion and concern, and to Cheryl, Susan, Lori and Todd—for their understanding and love—

CONTENTS

CONTENTS (Cont'd)

CONTENTS (Cont'd)

CONTENTS (Cont'd)

Congratulations! As a teacher aide actively engaged in the classroom or as someone interested in joining the profession, you are involved in one of the newest and most exciting educational occupations. The challenge of this new career will add a dynamic dimension to your life!

In the beginning you may have many apprehensions, fears, misgivings and generally "second thoughts" about this new venture. The challenge of newness alone gives rise to fear and doubt. However, these gnawing and questioning doubts should serve as factors of encouragement, for any person who seeks new challenges without these apparent apprehensive doubts is doomed to failure from the start. To be a good teacher aide, you must have basic concerns, doubts and apprehensions for nowhere in our educational structure is there room for smugness, apathy or self-satisfied complacency.

INTRODUCTION

Educators have generated many ideas directing both positive and negative approval towards the use of teacher aides in our educational system. However, the rewards and penalties of the teacher aide concept cannot be realistically evaluated or assessed until it becomes an ordered structural operation. It is unrealistic and foolhardy for any individual or school system to attempt to initiate or evaluate a teacher aide program while operating in a disordered or unstructured manner, especially if the system is formulated upon a tenuous foundation.

A vast majority of contemporary teacher aide programs cannot be realistically assessed due to their nebulous operating procedures. At present there are no accepted concrete teacher aide program models that can officially be considered a standard for comparison.

It is hoped that this text will clarify or cause to be taken into account many pertinent issues involving the employment and deployment of teacher aides. It is further hoped that this textual information will be discussed and given fair consideration when initially planning and organizing any type of teacher aide program.

Basically, the information compiled in this text is designed to provide background and procedural and operational information for teacher aides. It is your interpretation of this material as an aide, coupled with that of your administrators and teaching staff which actually will make possible and provide the necessary insight needed to give impetus, structure, order, and merit to future teacher aide programs.

You, as a teacher aide today, are a pioneer in a new educational dimension, and as in all new movements, you, the pioneer teacher aide, will be forced to undergo many trials and tribulations in making this program better for your successors. Your

1

involvement in this program can be expressed in the words of John Gardner when he said: "In a world that is rocking with change we need more than anything else a high capacity for adjustment to changed circumstances, a capacity for innovations."

CHAPTER I

AN OVERVIEW AND INTRODUCTION TO THE TEACHER AIDE PROGRAM

OURS IS an age which needs creative capacities in a wide variety of fields—an age in which adaptivity to social change and flexibility in meeting life's challenges need to be cultivated from earliest childhood to maturity.

Laura Zirbes

An Overview and Introduction to the Teacher Aide Program

Why Would I Want to be a Teacher Aide?

You must answer this question personally. However, the primary requisite for becoming a good teacher aide is a sincere desire to help children obtain the best education possible by providing optimum conditions in which the students can obtain that education.

A qualified person with a desire and some free time can generally become a volunteer teacher aide. The hours during which school is in session are desirable for any working person and as a volunteer you could arrange even better hours—those which fit your personal time schedule.

Most school districts are developing liberal salary schedules with fringe benefits for paid teacher aides. This factor, in addition to desirable hours, attracts many to the field of teacher assistance.

Time on your hands? Retired or just beginning your job career? Children grown and out of your home during the day? Regardless of your reason, if you have decided it is time for you to leave home during the day, employment as a teacher aide gives you an opportunity to explore the world in a way which gives your life new direction and dimension. Stimulating adult conversation coupled with an environment of youthful vigor will give you a new outlook on your life and your new career outside of your home along with your association with these energizing youth and innovative professionals may serve as a motivating stimulus for future endeavors.

What is the Present Definition of a Teacher Aide?

Educational literature describing teacher aides contains a great deal of conflicting and nondescriptive terminology. Many occupational titles given to persons who are designated to relieve teachers of various sundry tasks are relatively shallow and nebulous. Teacher aides, as an entity and as described in past and contemporary literature, escape any one meaningful definition.

For our purposes, we may define a teacher aide as a person who enters the school or classroom situation to attend to primarily non-instructional tasks and to serve as an observer and resource person for the teacher with all these tasks directed toward the goal of providing the opportunity for optimal education for all children.

Are Teacher Aides Really Needed?

Yes, expanded curricula, reorganization of the structured patterns in schools, differentiated roles for teachers, group work, seminar work and individualized instruction have made teaching a more complex and demanding job. There is an acute shortage of professional teachers available to meet the growing demands in today's classrooms and the implementation of auxiliary personnel is one way to effectively meet these mounting demands.

Auxiliary classroom personnel are not intended to replace teachers but to support and assist them in their increasingly complex role. The teacher is a skilled professional and as such must be permitted to operate at a professional level. A teacher should be a diagnostician first and secondly a director of learning experiences, the teacher should not be bogged down with routine trivia which could be effectively handled by a teacher aide.

The educational dilemma and crisis facing our nation must be met with new and imaginative ideas. The problems created by modern society, science and technology are new and to deal with them effectively there must be new solutions. Education is confronted with the fierce urgency of now.

Contemporary educational research finds many experimental projects seeking to develop new methodologies in which professional educators will be utilized more effectively and efficiently. These research projects are probing educational avenues for new ways in which teacher aides can be utilized to yield a greater number of benefits to students, instructors and aides.

Today's teachers must not only be better prepared, they must also prepare better than their predecessors. As an aide in the classroom you can help lighten the teacher load of ancillary and supervisional tasks and hence, give the teacher more time to prepare for and perform the instructional tasks. Educators agree that no teacher can be effective, regardless of how competent she is, unless she has the time to adequately prepare and present the classroom lessons.

Past and Present Use of the Teacher Aide Concept

Teacher aides are not a new educational innovation for teacher aide implementation is at least as old as planned education. But,

7

teacher aides, as implemented in the past and present, will not meet future educational needs.

The educational forecast indicates a continued and rapidly increasing demand for more efficiently planned use of the teacher's time as the throes of present educational policy-making fail to provide an environment in which a "hit or miss" auxiliary policy is satisfactory.

Paid teacher aides were first used extensively in the early 1940's. At this point in history, there was a serious teacher shortage along with a poor pay policy in our public schools, both due mainly to the depression of the 1930's. A third factor promoting the implementation of paraprofessionals was the need for the cost of professionals to train personnel to meet the needs of accelerating war industries. Aides were employed with a minimum of planning as an emergency measure and teachers met the war-time emergency aid with disgust and open hostility.

One of the next major attempts to employ teacher aides was the Bay City, Michigan project in 1952 sponsored by the Bay City schools and Central Michigan University made possible by a Ford Foundation grant.

The Bay City program was predicated on a continued teacher shortage. The aides served as an inducement for teachers to face the larger student-teacher ratios. The 1960's brought in a new era and a new, realistic aide program to meet the challenge of the classroom and changing needs of today's schools.

Present educational problems, spawned to greater awareness through professional negotiations, point to the need for better management of personnel to aid in practical adjustment of professional time to student needs.

It is the primary responsibility of the teacher to provide his students with the best possible education. To fulfill this responsibility, he must actively search for a stimulating learning atmosphere, a lively curriculum for all students and new approaches to instruction.

Various professional organizations espouse the above demands, seeking relief from the timeconsuming, nonproductive, routine duties through recognized and approved practices that are conducive to the educational movement in all respects. This, in substance, means having the relief come from a legally certified, organizationally approved and locally adopted semi-professional source.

Why the Sudden Emphasis on Teacher Aides?

Social, educational and economic factors have contributed to a sharp increase in the number of auxiliary personnel employed in schools and have evoked widespread interest in the development of the teacher aide concept. [1]

Prior to World War II, few paid teacher aides were employed. However, many of the certified teachers of that era would barely qualify as a certified aide today. During World War II teacher aides were employed as an emergency measure and the teachers were often openly hostile and negative toward aides. Teachers view aides with suspicion, distrust and as active usurpers of professionalism.

The non-teaching roles in schools, until the last two decades, were few consisting primarily of the school custodian, lunchroom personnel, truant officers, minimal office help and, if fortunate, a part-time nurse.

Reorganization of the structural patterns in schools, expanded curriculum, differentiated roles for teachers, cooperative and team

---

[1] *Auxiliary School Personnel: Their Roles, Training and Institutionalization*, based on a nationwide study conducted for the U.S. Office of Economic Opportunity, Bank Street College of Education, New York, October, 1966.

teaching, group work, seminar work, and individualized instruction have made teaching a more complex and demanding job. There is an acute shortage of professionals who cannot meet the growing needs and implementation of auxiliary personnel is one way to meet the increasing demand. Auxiliary personnel do not replace teachers, but they do support the teachers. [2]

Now one in every 100 American workers is employed on a public school institutional staff, serving as a teacher, principal, supervisor, librarian, guidance counselor, special service person or as a consultant.

According to a recent National Education Association research report [3] this sudden influx of auxiliary personnel involvement is due to the great advances in all dimensions of life. Today's teachers must not only be better prepared, they must also prepare better than their predecessors. The social, educational, economic and cultural systems have undergone radical changes in the last quarter century. These new dimensions demand that teachers devote their attention exclusively to their professional teaching responsibilities.

It also demands that auxiliary personnel be employed to attend to many of the superficial, time-consuming duties which over-burden teachers. Planned usage of auxiliary personnel is not to replace teachers, but to give them added strength and support so that they may become more proficient and efficient.

Why Specifically, a Non-Professional?

Because a teacher is a human being, she cannot know everything there is to know, do everything there is to do, nor play all the roles she is to play in a single school day. During the course of a child's educational experience he will have many

[2] Ibid.

[3] Estimates of School Statistics, 1967-68, National Education Association Research Report.

needs which the teacher is not capable of fulfilling, yet the student should have contact with persons who can and will satisfy his needs.

Many of the daily frustrations of the school-child seem trivial to his professional adult teacher whose primary aim is to teach. But to the child, new to the social world of school, even minor frustrations can be grossly exaggerated and misinterpreted. There is a need for an adult to smooth the way, an adult who is mediator between student and professional and the new world of expectations. The professional needs this mediator, too, to assume some of the trivial non-professional chores which are a part of the organizational day in school.

In contemporary school systems many functions which were primarily the responsibility of the professional teacher are being delegated to non-professionals because educators have learned that every moment a teacher spends on the non-instructional phases of her professional job is time she does not have to spend on her professional function.

In contemporary education a new leadership role is being developed for professional teachers that will help lessen the non-instructional work load. As the teacher assumes the managerial position and learns to coordinate the talents and manpower available from teacher aides, she will become the pivotal person, responsible and accountable for insuring that education occurs in the classroom. [4]

What is the Teacher-Teacher Aide Team Concept?

The concept of the instructional team has been defined as the extension of master teachers to supervisory direction of non-professional assistants in the classroom. The teacher is the

---

[4] Garda W. Bowman and Gordon J. Klopf, "New Careers and Roles in the American School." A study conducted for the Office of Economic Opportunity, New York: Bank Street College of Education, September, 1967, p.36-37, p. 153-154.

team leader and she has the responsibility of coordinating the educational growth of the whole child.

As an aide, the teacher will assign you tasks which will allow you to make a worthwhile contribution in the classroom yet not usurp the supervising teacher's professional power. Your introduction into the classroom situations will not reduce the teacher's actual teaching work load but it will give her more time to perform her professional functions.

Your supervising professional teacher is trained and certified to perform certain functions in the education of children such as the analysis of the instructional needs of the pupils and the initiation of educational activities to meet those needs. Since these are your supervising teacher's responsibilities, it is she who must inform you of your activities and the ideas behind them.

To feel that you are an integral part of the educational process you, as an aide, must be informed of the ideas behind the activities. By the supervising teacher's attitude and your inclusion or exclusion in planning activities, it is the teacher who makes or breaks the contributive role of the teacher aide.

The key to a successful teacher-teacher aide relationship is free communication based on flexibility of tasks and trust.

The attitude of an effective team approach is:

"Which of us can learn how to perform this particular task in a way that will give the most help to the greatest number of pupils?"

Do Aides Really Help Teachers do a Better Job of Teaching?

Yes . . . . by taking care of the time-consuming tasks normally performed by the teacher which do not require a college education, the aide gives her supervising teacher more time to prepare and to teach.

A teacher who utilizes her aide in an intelligent and professional manner may increase and strengthen her teaching role. A teacher aide in the classroom will not only give the teacher more time to plan and to teach, but will force the teacher to plan more specifically, realistically and thoroughly.

The amount of time needed for each teacher to use for teaching will depend basically on the individual teacher's ingenuity. The secret of freed teacher time rests in the degree of sophistication and resourcefulness used by each teacher in the assignment and deployment of aides.

In one research study it was found that a typical teacher can spend: [5]

89% less time - correcting papers
83% less time - monitoring written lessons
76% less time - taking attendance
61% less time - moving groups of pupils around
36% less time - disciplining pupils
25% less time - preparing reports

And she would have:

105% more time - to prepare lessons
57% more time - to hear recitations
41% more time - to supervise activities such as art, music and drama
27% more time - to help individual pupils at their desks
20% more time - to make and explain lesson assignments

Can a Teacher Aide Program Enhance and Stimulate an Entire School System?

An evaluative committee of educators has agreed that teacher aide programs tend to stimulate educational services in two

[5] *To What Extent Can Teacher Aides Free The Teacher's Time To Teach?* U.S. News and World Report, May 11, 1956.

ways: First, assuming normal professional competence on the part of the professional teacher, the aide program insures a better administered classroom with all necessary routines carefully monitored. Secondly, the aide program creates a demand for more services, such as instructional aides, by underscoring any deficiencies that may exist.[6]

A properly structured aide program offers an efficient, effective method of utilizing intelligent and highly competent individuals in an educational situation despite the fact that the aides may not have had professional teacher training.

Professional educators alone are not enough to insure academic success with all students. Aides can give teachers realistic knowledge of a community and assist the teacher in active involvement in the community which will bring the teacher a step closer to her students in bridging the communication gap.

An aide in the classroom gives students more adult attention which will enhance learning and bring about a warm social environment conducive to education.

What About Parental Opposition to a "Second-Class Education" Fostered by the Implementation of Teacher Aides?

When your employing school system began discussing the possibility of a teacher aide program, the administrators probably informed the parents of the community about the means, methods and goals of the program. Those parents who took the time to read about the program, ask questions and investigate its values will probably support you 100 per cent. However, there may be a few parents who will say that their children are being

---

[6] *A Cooperative Study for the Better Utilization of Teacher Competencies*, Final Evaluation Report, An Evaluative Report prepared by an Outside Evaluating Committee, Central Michigan University, Mt. Pleasant, Michigan, 1958, p. 27.

cheated. These parents will probably be those who are unaware of the purpose and function of a teacher aide.

Don't fight 'em—try to get them to join you. Explain firsthand and face-to-face just exactly how you function. Stress the fact that you do not teach the students but that you help the teacher by attending to non-instructional tasks so that the teacher will have more time to prepare and better present the lessons.

It is very important that each parent understand that you are not hired to teach per se. Explain that your service is not a supposition to increase classroom enrollments nor will it decrease the amount of individual student-teacher contact. Also, explain that with your service as an aide, the teacher will have more time for individual observation and instruction and that any duties that you may assume will be done only in accordance with your supervising teacher. It is difficult to separate exactly teaching functions, therefore it would be erroneous to say that you will not do any teaching. It should be made clear that you are not hired to replace teaching personnel in their professional duties, but to supplant them and to make their effort more realistic and meaningful to the students.

Schools employing teacher aides in a structured and proper manner are adding a plus factor to their students' education. Employment of teacher aides is one of the greatest deterrents to the ever increasing remedial education practices found so prevalent in today's educational systems.

The teacher aide concept is designed to provide preventative educational practices rather than contributing to rely on remedial educational practices. Parents should rightly be concerned about influences involving the educational training of their children. It is your duty to help school personnel inform parents of the merit and value of the teacher aide program, its objectives and its benefits.

CHAPTER II

*WHAT IS THE STRUCTURE, FUNCTION AND
PURPOSE OF THE TEACHER AIDE PROGRAM?*

THE teacher must now become a student of the community. She becomes a student of children as they grow up in the community and must constantly be appraising the impact of the total community upon the growth and development of individual children.

Ernest O. Melby

What is the Structure, Function and Purpose of the Teacher Aide Program?

Do Most Teacher Aide Programs Have a Definite Individual Structure, Function and Purpose?

For the implementation of any aide program it is necessary for the program to first be conceived and studied, then it must be made operable and answerable to a structured overall master aide employment-deployment plan. Proper planning is important for it will enhance the program's operable success and insure ease of entry with faster, sounder progress yielding more readily measurable achievements.

As an aide, whether full-time or part-time, volunteer or paid, you will operate best within a planned and enforced categorical structure. For optimum progress it is imperative that each type of aide program perform only the function for which it has been given order, structure and authority.

In the initial planning stages each school system will have taken into account the factors peculiar to its district and have decided which type aide program or programs would best meet its particular needs.

What Should be the Goals of a Teacher Aide Program?

Two basic goals of the teacher aide program should be to serve as an "Adult Out-Reach Program" and as a "Student In-Reach Program." The program should be structured to provide more child-adult contact within and without both the classroom and the school and to bring the adults of the community into the school.

An adult out-reach program could easily provide many new educational and social services. A program with this orientation could also provide for and result in new learning vistas previously unexplored in today's educational system.

The overriding aim of the program is to help teachers provide and interpret new, better, more meaningful and worthwhile educational insights to the youth entrusted to their care.

Routine duties properly delegated to the aide can free and enhance the instructor's time. Assignment of duties should be on an individual teacher-teacher aide team basis according to the aide's educational preparation, personal strengths, work experience and willingness to accept specific assignments.

The designation and delegation of tasks to an aide is bounded strictly by the aide's experience and education in conjunction with the teacher's managerial skills in coordinating a team effort.

What is the Purpose of the Teacher Aide Program?

It is hoped that through the implementation of teacher aide programs:

1) school systems will be able to attract and hold creative master teachers

2) educational institutions will be able to stress more positive, preventive methods, rather than propagating present methods which create a demand for remedial educative practices

3) a lower teacher-student contact ratio will come into existence and achieve a meaningful actuality and yield more individualized adult-student attention

4) teacher aides will be employed and encouraged in every school system regardless of their poverty or affluence. The teacher aide movement is a step toward greater community-school involvement and rapport will often be created through the use of sub-professional persons indigenous to the area

5) teacher aides, like all structured movements will take steps to improve organization at all levels, while teachers continue to guard their "territorial rights" with great zeal

6) teacher training institutions will become more exact in providing their trainees with knowledge to effectively and efficiently use their aides

7) the standard order of college course arrangement will undergo several changes, i.e., Human Growth and Development, as well as other disciplines, may come first rather than at the sophomore or junior level

8) professional teaching organizations will continue to demand lower teacher-student ratios as well as demand teacher aides

9) future aides will be selected for specific needs, rather than qualifications and ability

What is not the Purpose of a Teacher Aide Program?

When you enter the teacher aide program your sole purpose will be to enhance the overall learning environment of the school and help to provide the optimum educational benefits for the students in your assigned classroom.

It is extremely important that you understand that a teacher aide program is in no way intended to:

1) reduce or supplant the teaching staff

2) cut the cost of teaching

3) endanger teacher salary schedules

4) downgrade education

5) usurp the teacher's authority or classroom leadership

6) force teachers into unwanted or greater teaching loads

7) force teachers into becoming subject matter specialists

8) serve as a bargaining benefit in negotiation of teacher contracts

9) evaluate or judge the classroom teacher

10) provide insignificant and unrealistic jobs, solely to provide employment

CHAPTER III

WHAT ARE SOME VIEWS AND FUTURE TRENDS OF THE PRESENT TEACHER AIDE PROGRAM?

IF we help boys and girls learn the process of discovering knowledge and ways of working for themselves, we need not give our energies to finding fascinating ways to hold their attention or whip up their enthusiasm. The strong urge to pursue learning comes from within.

Lucile Lindberg, "Learning Through Searching," *Childhood Education*, October, 1961, pp. 58-60.

What are Some Views and Future Trends of the Present Teacher Aide Program?

How do Administrators View Teacher Aides?

In most cases teacher aides are greeted with open arms. You as a teacher aide are an asset, even though initially you may be viewed with distrust and considered an additional expense by both administrators and teachers.

Generally, contemporary educators agree that our present educational system is in need of a structured teacher aide program. They also agree that our society requires and will continue to require increasingly significant educational changes involving teacher aides. Educational policy-making can no longer provide an environment in which a "hit-or-miss" auxiliary teacher help policy is satisfactory. The educational forecast indicates a continued and rapidly growing need for a more efficiently planned use of the teacher's time.

Reorganization of the structural patterns in schools, expanded curriculum, differentiated roles for teachers, cooperative and team teaching, group work, seminar work and individualized instruction have made teaching a more complex and demanding job. There is an acute shortage of professionals who cannot meet the growing needs and the implementation of teacher aides is one way to meet the increasing demands made on the professional's time.

Social, educational, economic and cultural structures have all undergone radical changes in the last quarter century and demand new solutions and improvements. These new dimensions demand that teachers devote more of their attention to their professional teaching responsibilities exclusively. It also demands that auxiliary personnel be employed to attend to many of the superficial, time-consuming duties which do not command a professional's attention but presently overburden the teachers. Well-informed administrators realize that planned usage of auxiliary personnel is not designed to replace teachers but to give teachers added strength and support to enable them to become more proficient and efficient in their professional roles.

How do Educational "Purists" View the Use of Teacher Aides?

Looking upon teacher aides as flagrant violators of sound educational principles, educational purists view the teacher aide concept with contempt.

Believing that aides will usurp power and undermine the authority role of teachers, purists view teacher aides as unscrupulous invaders whose sole purpose is to exploit, plagiarize and contaminate the sound time-tested values of education. Purists feel the use of teacher aides is, with impunity, a gross violation of the traditional role reserved for the classroom teacher.

Even though you, as an aide, are assigned a supportive role and you clearly understand that your role is secondary and

limited, purists still believe that you will be a constant potential
threat. They feel that your introduction into the classroom as
an aide places the teacher in a position of either consciously or
unconsciously vying with another adult, who may unwittingly
serve as a competitive adult force in the classroom.

Purists also say that students are forced to choose between
teacher and aide power positions on individual matters while
at the same time being in a position of either consciously or
unconsciously creating events and situations that pit one adult
power-figure against the other.

Once a teacher feels her position of authority is threatened,
a great deal of her teaching time will be spent in rationalization
and defensive activities. A basic defensive action is explanation
and justification of classroom activities to her assigned aide.
Purists feel that since few teachers are conditioned and trained
in the use and management of teacher aides, their knowledge
will limit and restrict teacher-student contact as the teacher
herself is directed toward compulsory and perfunctory obligations.

Has the Federal Government Encouraged Teacher Aide Programs?

Yes, the Elementary and Secondary Education Act of 1965
provided many school districts with funds for employment
of teacher aides to assist with programs designed to help culturally deprived children. In 1965 the U.S. Office of Education
provided written guidelines which suggested use of sub-
professional personnel in assisting teachers in educating culturally deprived students. [1]

The guidelines emphasize two basic reasons for hiring teacher
aides: (1) to provide a vital and realistic service to the schools,

---

[1] *Guidelines for Special Programs for Educationally Deprived Children*, Department of Health,
Education and Welfare, Office of Education, Draft, October 5, 1965, p. 20.

teachers, students, community and parents and (2) to serve as a positive effort in bridging the communication gap between home and school.

Educational research continually indicates that parents in many areas feel isolated or ignored by their local schools. In order to combat this, Title I, ESEA, has established the criteria which cause parents to have a larger voice in determining the educational programs and services to be provided their children. Parental involvement is stressed through home-school visits, parent education classes, field trips and conferences, with the employment of the parents as either paid or volunteer aides emphasized.

In 1967 the Education Professional Bill [2] made it possible for state education agencies to submit state plans which would include programs utilizing teacher aides. These plans would also provide pre-service and in-service training designed to enable aides to better perform their duties. This act forces state educational agencies to move on the use of teacher aides if the state receives federal funds.

How Widespread is the Use of Teacher Aides?

Today there are approximately 200,000 teacher aides working in schools throughout the United States and it is estimated that there will be two million teacher aides employed by 1975.

Educational Research Service indicated that during the 1965-66 school year, of 217 surveyed school systems in New York utilizing aides, the aides served a total of 400,000 hours each week in elementary schools.

---

[2] Education Profession Act, P.L. 90-35 Sec. 520, Title V, Part B., Higher Education Act of 1965, amended.

What are Some Views and Future Trends of the Present Teacher Aide Program?

The New York State Department of Education took a survey of teacher aides in the fall of 1965 [3] which indicated that 428 of the 629 school districts in the state, or 68 per cent, were using teacher aides.

Of the 428 districts now using aides, only ten have used them in excess of ten years. Twenty-three employed aides for the first time in 1965-66.

Nearly half of the teacher aide programs now operating in large public schools are less than three years old. A sampling of large school districts found that 40 per cent of all large teacher aide programs were started in the 1965-66 school year and 36 per cent between 1960 and 1964. [4]

A survey by the National Educational Research Division (NEA) revealed that one of five public school teachers have some type of teacher aide program. Of these, 14 per cent share the services of one or more aides with other teachers, 5 per cent have the exclusive service of one or more aides.

All sizes and types of school systems use teacher aides. Researchers found no significant difference between the proportion of teachers in small systems to the proportion in large school systems, but research has shown that geographically, there are more teachers in the west utilizing teacher aides than in any other region of the United States.

One day auxiliary personnel may outnumber teachers. The trend toward more extensive use of teacher aides is evidenced by the New England Assessment Project which reported that

---

[3] *Teacher Aides in Large School Systems,* Educational Research Service Circular, No. 2, 1967, Washington, D.C., The Association, April, 1967, NEA Stock No. 219-06234, p. 1-2.

[4] *Survey of Public School Teacher Aides,* State Education Department, University of the State of New York, Bureau of School and Cultural Research, Albany, The Departmental, April, 1966.

teacher aides have increased in New England (Maine - 21%, Connecticut - 22%, Massachusetts - 46%, New Hampshire - 4%, Rhode Island - 4% and Vermont - 3%) from 12 school systems employing aides in 1960 to 230 systems in 1967.

Aides are a significant factor in education in New England and their number will increase as education associations encourage their employment and the Federal Government provides funds for payment of their salaries through the program. The aides are performing tasks that are ancillary to instruction, thus providing the teacher with more time for preparation and presentation of instructional activities in the classroom. [5]

In What Size Schools are Teacher Aides Used Most Efficiently?

The size of the school has little direct bearing on the feasibility and implementation of the teacher aide program. The success of the teacher aide program rests on five basic factors:

1) the overall acceptance of the aide program within and without the school system

2) the means of aide employment and deployment

3) the type and quality of supervision

4) planned in-service upgrading

5) understanding of the duties to be performed and of the qualifications required at each level.

Small school systems as well as large systems can utilize teacher aides effectively. No significant difference exists between

---

[5] *Teacher Aides in the Classroom*, A Digest, A New England Study Prepared by the New England Educational Assessment Project, A Cooperative Regional Report of the Six New England States, Providence, Rhode Island, 1967, p. 8.

the proportion of teachers in small systems and large school systems who reported using aides (see *"How Widespread is the Use of Teacher Aides?").* In your role as an aide, the size of the school should have little, if any, direct bearing on your tasks or proficiency. Geographically, more teachers in the West than in other regions of the country have the services of teacher aides. [6]

In the school year 1967-68, 743 school systems reported using 29,938 teacher aides. There were 2,878 aides used in kindergarten or pre-primary schools, 18,599 in elementary schools, 3,400 in junior high schools, 4,973 in senior high schools and 48 special aides or aides whose assignment was not specified.

For the school year 1968-69, there were 40,295 teacher aides employed in 799 school systems of enrollments of 6,000 or more. Of these 5,049 were in kindergarten or pre-primary schools, 25,131 in elementary schools, 3,951 in junior high schools, 4,957 in senior high schools and 1,208 were special aides or their assignments were not specified. [7]

What Trends are Developing in the Use of Teacher Aides?

In considering aide employment you will be particularly interested in knowing that:

1) Teacher aides are becoming more involved in the entire educational process.

2) Contemporary teacher aides most often find themselves in blighted urban schools and high poverty impact

---

[6] "How the Profession Feels About Teacher Aides," *Teacher Opinion Poll,* NEA Journal, Vol. 56, No. 8, November, 1967.

[7] NEA Research Bulletin, Vol. 47, No. 2, May, 1969.

areas. This may be attributed to the fact that the Federal Government gives these areas high priority in both service and financial renumeration.

3) Successful teacher aide programs are forcing a structured order of the teacher aide employment group. This gives aide employment benefits and security.

4) Federal, state and local governments are becoming more active in their support of teacher aide programs.

5) Educational institutions are now providing various types of training for teacher aides—with sound guidance criteria. The previously nebulous nature of teacher aides aided and abetted the contemporary training confusion. Current trends show emerging formalized programs. Junior colleges are and will continue to be the authority for teacher aides as they develop programs that will fit every structured aide category.

6) Teachers are viewing teacher aides in an increasingly positive and supportive manner.

7) Parents and communities are dropping the "second class" tag and are viewing the teacher aide programs as valuable assets to the educational system.

8) Teacher aide employment is fast becoming a good way for adults to enter or re-enter the labor force.

9) The teacher aide movement is becoming a realistic and practical manner in which to bring about job up-grading to the teaching profession and the aide employment group while increasing the status of the professional teacher.

CHAPTER IV

**WHAT PROCEDURES ARE INVOLVED IN THE
SELECTION OF TEACHER AIDES?**

THE teacher must be constantly in touch with the everchanging American life — its needs, conditions, trends, practices, knowledge, aspirations. There is no such thing as a "completed" education for the truly effective teacher in an American public school.

Harl R. Douglass

What Procedures are Involved in the Selection of Teacher Aides?

Who Makes the Selection of Persons for Teacher Aide Employment?

According to research findings by New York State Teachers Association, 83 per cent of the state districts surveyed which are employing teacher aides reported that the job of selecting aides was done by one or more members of the administrative staff, with teachers and administrators acting cooperatively in 7 per cent of the districts. It has also been reported that more than 50 per cent of the districts' methods of hiring and deployment practices were suggested by the administrator.

In 41 per cent of the cases studied, individual teachers and teacher groups cooperatively planned with the administration. Cooperative planning efforts resulted in teachers either initiating employing plans or developing guide lines for employment practices.

Generally the employment and deployment of all teacher aide personnel is the responsibility of the district school administrator and is primarily determined by the prevailing local structure, conditions and needs.

The supervising teacher who is expected to work with and be responsible for the aide should take an active part in the final interview and selection process. Ideally, the supervising teacher should play an active role in selecting her aide. This practice appears to be a spiraling practice in aide selection procedures.

What are the Educational Expectations for Prospective Teacher Aides?

To a large degree this depends upon the aide classification in which you are seeking aide employment.

For classifications such as mother and father aides, education is not as important as is a sincere desire to help young children. For a classification such as reader-grader aide you will need at least a high school diploma and some college, if not a college degree.

You will need specific types of training for certain aide classifications. Specifically, a person may have a degree in chemistry but unless he has some training in literature and composition he will not be a qualified, effective reader-grader aide.

Generally, basic aide training and indoctrination will be handled by the individual school system. This will include clarification of your position, your relation to the school staff, resources available and in some school systems, basic education courses on a college level.

Should There be an Educational Ceiling Placed on Teacher Aide Applicants?

School working conditions and the typical school calendar make the aide job attractive, convenient and desirable for many people, including many of those who are highly trained. These are only a few of the many reasons why you as a well-qualified person may desire to serve as a teacher aide. Former teachers who do not wish to teach full-time may fill special teacher aide slots very well, while others may accept a non-professional role with various long-range professional objectives in mind.

However, it is wise for both you and the interviewer to question your motives as a well-qualified person seeking an aide position. For the teacher must feel secure, undisturbed and unchallenged by the other adult in her classroom and not everyone who has experienced leadership can revert to a passive, follower role.

You must realize that by accepting a teacher aide position you will be under the direct supervision of the teacher. As a teacher aide you can not make plans to revamp the school system and then go ahead with your plans. You are an aide, an aide only, not a supervisor and you must receive directions rather than give them. This reversal of roles is often very difficult to do, this is the reasoning backing the review of reasons for the highly qualified person seeking aide employment.

I Have Lived Here for Twenty Years, Will I be Given Preference in the Selection Process?

Yes . . . . it is quite likely that you will be given preference because you are from a background similar to that of the parents and community, and in so being you are able to perceive, discuss and deal with the people and the problems of the community in an informed manner.

In the school system problems can easily be heightened or diminished according to the referent value system used. This is particularly true in the disadvantaged neighborhood where as an indigenous person you may be able to display more rapport with and sensitivity to the students and parents than the teacher or the school community are able to develop.

Because you are indigenous to the area you will be able to interpret community mores in a way which will give educators better, more meaningful and realistic insights in which to temper their judgments and actions. The greater the deviation from the middle class value system, either up or downward, the greater the need for employing you as an indigenous aide. Properly selected and trained, you will be helpful in inspiring teachers to provide a more meaningful and effective learning environment.

However, do not rely on this one factor to serve as your strong point. Indigenousness is an asset but there are many assets ranked higher.

Should Persons on Welfare and Relief Roles be Assigned to Work as Teacher Aides?

If you are on Welfare or relief roles do not expect to be hired strictly on the basis of your financial need. Regardless of the type of aide category, you will be employed strictly on the basis of your merit and ability to make a worthwhile contribution to some part of the educational program.

Just being a poor and available person, indigenous to the community is not sufficient criteria for being hired as a teacher aide at any categorical level. The only persons who should be hired are those whom initial planning allows for and provides for accordingly to become an integral part of the overall operation.

Stereotyping the poor, ignorant or indigent has occasionally caused the aide program some unfavorable comments and temporary setbacks. However, there is no valid reason to qualify or disqualify any person solely on the basis of his economic status.

The largest potential pool of sub-professional talent has been found in the low-income groups which have supplied teacher aides under the recent educational programs for combating poverty. America's low-income areas have benefited most from the use of aides in their schools. In the summer of 1964, some 46,000 teacher aides were used in preschool programs in low-income areas throughout the country.[1]

What Qualities do Interviewers Look for in Screening Teacher Aides?

Because of your association with the school in the aide capacity, and as such, your example to school children and the community, you must be of very strong character.

You must be in good physical health and you will probably be required to show proof of a negative tuberculin test. It is also desirable that you pass a routine physical examination.

In evaluation the interviewer should ask himself: "Is this the kind of person I would want to be in a position to exert constant influence on my child?" A strong effective teacher aide program is not the result of good fortune, but only the result of good planning. Critical areas which should be thoroughly investigated when selecting aides are:

1) patience and tolerance
2) restraint in the use of crude and abusive language
3) restrained philosophy on the use of physical force and coercion
4) willingness to accept responsibility
5) fondness for children
6) friendliness
7) honesty, integrity and sincerity
8) cooperativeness
9) respect for individual differences and personal worth

---

[1] William J. Rioux, "At The Teacher's Right Hand," *American Education*, December 1965 - January 1966, p. 5-6.

10) appropriate philosophies on empathy, apathy, authority and permissiveness
11) appropriate manner of dress and general personal neatness
12) restraint of personal bias and prejudice
13) restraint of personal points of contention and areas of criticism
14) philosophy of leadership and/or followership
15) demonstrated sensitivity to the needs of youth
16) ability to work with a teacher-supervisor
17) ability to work with various school personnel

CHAPTER V

WHAT ABOUT THE TRAINING OF TEACHER AIDES?

Education is the leading of human souls to what is best, and making what is best out of them; and these two objects are always attainable together, and by the same means. The training which makes men happiest in themselves also makes them most serviceable to others.

John Ruskin: *Stones of Venice*, 1853.

What About the Training of Teacher Aides?

Who Will Give me my Training?

Generally, you will be given your indoctrination and training within the school system and possibly within the school in which you will be employed. Training sessions may be conducted by administrators, teachers in the system or specific persons assigned to train and indoctrinate teacher aides.

Some school systems have a program with local community colleges to train aides to the specific school system's specifications. In some cases aides may earn college transferable credit.

Although you may be receiving your training on a college campus, in most cases you will not matriculate, but enroll in a special program coordinating school system and college efforts. If you have not been able to gain admittance to a college previously, this college experience may help you to later gain regular admittance to a college.

Many times the college credit which an aide can earn will be transferred to a college in which she may matriculate. Some of the teacher aide programs at junior colleges are designed to enable the aide to earn transferable credits. This serves as an inducement for the aide to seek higher education. One of the greatest benefits of the structured teacher aide program is its ability to offer advancement and upward mobility opportunities.

What Kind of Training do I Need?

Regardless of your aide capacity, you will benefit from both pre-service and in-service follow-up training. Since harmony in working relationships is so important, guidelines for your actions and those of your supervising teachers must be set up.

Points that should be stressed in indoctrination are: 1) Professionalism . . . all aides will have varying amounts of access to privileged professional information. You must realize that as an aide you operate on the same basis of ethics as the teaching profession. 2) Behavior . . . exemplary behavior on the part of the aide certainly is important because of your constant exposure to children in the classroom. 3) Cooperation . . . team work and harmony are vital to the success of the program. 4) Punctuality . . . educational activities are generally time-oriented and punctuality is a basic key to success. 5) Responsibility . . . to explain all of the encompassing demands and types of responsibilities found in a school system.

In addition to this your aide training should include experience for the particular job you will be doing. This may be accomplished through a *work-experience program* which gives you, as a prospective aide, the opportunity to achieve techniques and develop practices which have relevance to your particular job assignment. The learning by doing theory is directly applied on the job in role playing and job simulation techniques.

Some school districts have formal in-service training programs for aides to foster the development of skills in working with students, teachers and staff. This program is planned to develop your proficiency as an aide and to encourage your personal development of the role to be played in classroom human relations.

A formal in-service training program might include: [1]

1) Basic Communications: fundamentals of grammar and composition

2) Basic Mathematics: a short course in modern math to help you, the aide, become familiar with the course of study and the text and materials to be used

3) Audio-Visual Techniques and Machine Operations: to give you an opportunity to develop skills in the use of mimeograph, ditto, tape recorder, motion picture projector, slide projector, and other audio-visual aids

4) Child Development: an introduction to the growth, development and social development of the elementary school child

5) Resource Centers: to acquaint the aide with resources available

6) Elementary School Procedures: to acquaint the aide with procedures involved in regard to scheduling, the building, records and other formal procedures and followed in the assigned school.

Some school districts have college programs which lead to certification of the aide as well as giving the aide college experience which may encourage her to continue her education.

---

[1] *A Look at Teacher Aides and Their Training,* Metropolitan Educational Research Association, Michigan State University, East Lansing, Michigan, 1968, p. 8.

The degree of formality of the aide training program will depend on the structure and degree of sophistication of the individual aide program.

There is a need for every aide who is hired and a need for a training program for every aide. You should not fear the training requirement because its sole purpose is to help you better perform your job.

Is it Absolutely Necessary That I Receive Some Specific Classroom-Oriented Training?

Yes . . . regardless of your duties or assignments you should be required to attend at least two in-service training sessions to ease your entry into the classroom.

The minimal training sessions should focus on the school's basic educational objectives and policies and the manner in which the teacher aides themselves will be involved.

Follow-up sessions would be to answer your questions of "why," "what," "where," "what for," "who," and "when." In these follow-up sessions, past teacher aide experience should be discussed with consideration for future courses of action.

It is unfair to expect an aide to perform at peak efficiency from the start. You need indoctrination and training to help you with your role in school involvement. You must be aware of the fact that once you are identified with school service and the teaching profession, you must assume the responsibilities of your new role. You are required to adopt a standard of behavior commensurate with your position and worthy of respect from the teachers, the students and the community. To be meaningful, in-service training should be designed to provide added measures of assurance and insurance to the successful operation of a teacher aide program.

What is Stressed in Training?

All aides, regardless of their capacity, will benefit from both pre-service and in-service training. Since harmony in working

46

High school student aides instructing.

Teacher aides instructing young children.

relationships is so important, guidelines for the actions of both teachers and aides must be understood and maintained.

In your aide training program you can expect these points to be stressed:

Professionalism — all aides will have varying amounts of access to privileged professional information. You must realize that as an aide you operate on the same basis of ethics as the teaching profession.

Behavior — exemplary behavior on the part of the aide certainly is important

Cooperation — team work and harmony are vital to the success of the program

Punctuality — educational activities are generally time-oriented and punctuality is a basic key to success

Responsibility — to explain all of the encompassing demands and types of responsibilities found in a school system

CHAPTER VI

**WHAT ARE THE EMPLOYMENT CONDITIONS
FOR TEACHER AIDES?**

It is where understanding and shared purpose have been built into a going relationship that life feels good at each day's return.

Harry and Bonaro Overstreet

What are the Employment Conditions for Teacher Aides?

As an Aide Will I be Employed Full or Part Time?

To a large degree, this depends on you. If you are a volunteer aide you may work as many hours as is convenient for both you and the employing school.

If you are a paid aide, you will most likely work a full school day. Since the paid aide program is more structured, you will be under more supervision and will be given more explicit direction by the employing school, which in turn will have the right to expect your presence at the designated hours.

Some service or social organizations volunteer the services of their members, either collectively or individually. Individuals in this type of service program spend from one to ten hours per week in the schools, depending upon personal and school schedules.

Whether you commit yourself to either a paid or volunteer program, you have a responsibility to be in school the hours designated and to perform the designated duties. To be an effective volunteer aide or an effective paid teacher aide, you must care enough to do your very best.

What are Paid Teacher Aides?

A paid teacher aide is any person within a school system who is legally and specifically employed to assist certified teachers in discharging their teaching and ancillary duties and is paid for her services.

A paid teacher aide is usually assigned to a specific school and hopefully to a specific teacher. The paid aide program is more rigidly structured than the volunteer aide program due to the renumeration control factor. When giving a verbal commitment or signing a contract, paid aides commit themselves to presence at specified times and performance of duties at the capability level expected by the employing school personnel.

The paid aide will probably be hired to perform a specific duty for a specific teacher or teachers, such as grading papers, giving art instructions, aiding a physical education teacher, helping a chemistry teacher supervise laboratory work, supervising study halls, playgrounds, the lunchroom and monitoring the halls.

Paid aides will be found in various school systems, generally performing the essential but non-teaching tasks which are in many schools still the duties of the professional teacher.

Will Paid Teacher Aide Programs Cost the School Systems More Money?

Initially the employment of teacher aide personnel will require increased expenditures by local school systems. However,

54

federal legislation has been passed which gives financial consideration to schools for the employment of teacher aides. Federal legislation for teacher aides is predicated on five basic factors:

1) it allows more meaningful employment

2) it serves as an encouraging step to individuals seeking occupational upgrading

3) it allows educational institutions to better meet contemporary student needs

4) it emphasizes a positive or preventive approach more desirable than the remedial program

5) in long-range planning, good education costs less per student than poor education.

Future educational legislation and financial appropriations will be predicated on the program's acceptance and its overall success.

In judging costs, the time factor must be taken into consideration. Short-range educational planning will find that a paid teacher aide program will increase the per-pupil educational cost. The reasons for the additional costs are the same as those found in all short-range programs. Time is an economizing factor in program costs. Long-range educational planning will find that the paid aide program will decrease the overall, per-pupil educational cost.

New methods and improvements in any area generally involve higher costs. Although money is a prime factor and an expediter of miracles, the initial cost outlay should not be the sole dictator of the merits of the teacher aide program. The most important question is whether the advantages gained from paid teacher aides are worth the additional cost. This can be judged on the basis of two questions:

1) Will teacher aides prevent waste of time, money and resources which occur when professional teachers are encumbered and/or prevented from fully developing and maximizing their potential?

2) Will the use of aides bring about conditions more conducive to better teaching, greater educational benefits to the student-teacher relationships, and a lower rate of teacher turnover?

How are Teacher Aides Rewarded?

There are four basic factors which are usually considered in determining renumeration for teacher aides:

1. aide classification
2. hours of employment
3. conditions of employment
4. type of deployment

Volunteer aides are rewarded with the personal satisfaction they derive from giving service and help to you and the heartfelt "thank you" of the students and teachers.

Student aides are rewarded in a number of ways:

1. an enriching experience

2. as fulfillment of a service club or future teachers club task assignment

3. as a means of working out school fees

4. as a unit credit towards graduation

5. at a minimal paid hourly rate

Paid aide wages vary from \$1.25 to \$5.00 per hour. Aides generally work a six-hour day and perform their duties only while the students are in school.

Paid special aides receive all types of renumeration, including command of the highest teacher aide financial benefits, commensurate with their training and ability. The salary range for special aides is from $2.00 to $5.00 per classroom hour.

Practical aide and certified aide pay scales vary from $1.25 to $2.60 per hour.

Reader-grader aides are often paid on a piecework scale. Per-page rates for reader-grader aides range from $.15 to $.35. This rate varies with the prevailing area wage rates and the length and type of paper.

Hourly rates are generally preferred over the piecework method by many educators for various personal and professional reasons. Hourly rates for reader-grader aides range from $1.50 to $3.50 with anything over $3.50 considered an exception.

Reader-grader aides may also be employed as resource tutors or for conferences. The rates for these services range from $2.00 to $5.00 per hour. The advanced training and screening requirement for reader-grader aides accounts for the substantial wage differential.

A New York State Teachers Association survey showed the median hourly pay rate for the New York City area to be $2.25 per hour as compared to up-state New York where the median hourly rate was $1.67 per hour. This supports the commonly held supposition that higher pay is available in larger cities.

Some school districts have placed their aides on annual contracts while others are strictly hourly. The most stable situation occurs where the aide is committed to work each day that school is in session, for the length of the school day.

In February of 1969 the Union School District of Jackson, Michigan, which employs 99 teacher aides, gave the aide classifications the same fringe benefit package given to maintenance, custodial and cafeteria personnel. '

This package included:

a) a fully paid hospitalization insurance program for aides and their families

b) a $2,000 term life insurance policy

c) one paid sick day per month for each month of employment

d) eight paid vacation days per year

e) five paid vacation days per year

Although teacher aide personnel did not join either of the unions representing the maintenance, custodial and cafeteria personnel, they were arbitrarily placed in this group by school administrators to avoid a third negotiating force.

The Jackson Public Schools teacher aide salary schedule is as follows:

Classi-fication	Pay Basis	Minimum 1st yr.	Next Year	Next Year	Next Year	Maximum 5th year	8 yrs. Total 1 yr. at Max.	15 yrs. Total & 1st Rate
5	Hourly	$1.99	$2.08	$2.18	$2.28	$2.39	$2.50	$2.63
7	Hourly	2.18	2.28	2.39	2.50	2.62	2.74	2.88
8	Hourly	2.28	2.39	2.50	2.62	2.74	2.88	3.02
9	Hourly	2.39	2.50	2.62	2.74	2.88	3.00	3.15

Teacher Aide classifications are:

5 Teacher-Aide I — Non-High School Graduate

7 Teacher-Aide II — High School Graduate and up to 60 semester hours of college credit

---

' Clarence Lacny, Utilizing Teacher Aides in the Jackson, Michigan, Public Schools, "A Dual Opportunity," Jackson Public Schools, 1970.

(7) (Matron Attendant for Special Education)

8   — High School Graduate and Teacher Aide Certificate from Jackson Community College

9 Teacher Assistant — More than 60 semester hours of college credit

Fringe benefits are included for all these classifications.

What is the Legal Employment Status of Teacher Aides?

Each state has its specific certification laws which specifically state the minimal qualifications for persons desiring employment as teachers in schools. Therefore, unless there are specific statutes providing for other means, a teacher aide is not authorized to perform instructional duties or to teach. [2]

The Education Professions Development Act provides pre-service or in-service training of aides which will enable them to be better aides. In order to participate in this program, the state must have a designated program of state supervision and leadership for the development of policies and procedures on the use of federal funds to obtain and train teacher aides.

Because most states do not have specific statutory provisions pertaining to teacher aides, there have been instances in which the power of school boards has been challenged. However, judicial authority has generally supported the premise that, in the absence of statutes to the contrary, the power to hire and pay teacher aides is within the authority of local school districts.

---

[2] Kentucky, O.A.C., No. 269-1963.

In a Minnesota legal battle over the employment of a school nurse, the court said:

> "The purpose of a corporation is to maintain efficient free public schools . . . and, unless expressly restricted, (the school board) necessarily possesses the power to employ such persons as are required to accomplish the purpose." [3]

Other courts have held that the board has the authority to determine the mode and course of instruction.

To avoid challenged power, some state legislatures have recently enacted statutes providing for the employment of teacher aides. Not all statutes are comprehensive and explicitly detailed, but they do give the employment of teacher aides a legal basis. In other states, state boards of education and state departments of education have released statements specifying the use of aides in the public schools. These statements do not carry the weight of law, but they do imply direction and guidance in the employment and deployment of teacher aides.

Giving legal sanction to the aide program are legislatively enacted programs such as the Elementary and Secondary Education Act of 1965 which provides many school districts with the necessary funds to employ teacher aides to assist in programs designed for culturally deprived children.

What are the Legal Responsibilities of Teacher Aides?

Regardless of your employment or deployment capacity, whether paid or unpaid, you as a teacher aide should adhere to all the legal requirements applicable to any other school employee.

---

[3] State V. Brown, 112 Minn., 370, 128 N.W. 294.

When teacher aides are assigned tasks involving supervision, they are placed in positions of potential liability for pupil injury. In such a situation, liability is likely to arise out of negligence on the part of the aide. Any person assigned such responsibilities is ignorant at his own peril. If he is not qualified to supervise playgrounds, etc., he should not try to do so.

In cases involving pupil injury the courts have traditionally held the teacher to a higher standard of care than that owed to the general public. Likewise, a teacher aide when placed in a supervisory capacity owes the pupils a greater standard of care than is normally required in other personal relationships. [4]

Legal questions involving civil actions should not become an issue if you perform your aide duties diligently and under the general supervision of a legally certified educator. However, precautionary planning measures must be taken. Every action performed by school personnel must be predicated on sound judgment and substantiated by the use of reasonable care and prudence.

In your position as an aide, you should fully understand your legal status and responsibility before assuming your job. *Do not assume you are given blanket protection in all assigned situations.* Ignorance of the law and assumptions serve only as rationalization, not as substantiated legality.

For a detailed explanation of responsibilities see the section on aide classification and duties.

---

[4] S. Kern Alexander, "What Teacher Aides Can-And Cannot—Do," *Nation's Schools*, Vol. 82, No. 2, August, 1968.

Will I be Admitted to Teacher Staff Meetings?

This will depend upon your status as a teacher aide in the school and in the individual classroom in which you are employed.

If you are not a part of the teacher-teacher aide team concept, the teacher may resent your presence at the meeting and see it as an infringement upon her professional territory. In cases where this is true, aides should not be invited to the teaching staff meetings at the risk of alienating the professional teacher and arousing hostilities.

Because information is best obtained firsthand, in cases where a teacher-teacher aide team exists, teacher, aide and students would all benefit from the aide's presence at teaching staff meetings.

Many ideas and policies are drawn and shaped in teaching staff meetings on the basis of exchange of classroom experience. Because you, as an aide, have also had this classroom experience and especially because you have had these experiences in a new dimension, you should be allowed to watch the formation of new ideas and, upon invitation of the staff, take an active, contributive part in teaching staff meetings.

If you, as an aide, are invited to teaching staff meetings, you should attend. If you are not invited, you should encourage professionals to see the value of your experience as a contributor at these meetings.

The contemporary teacher aide movement is a new concept, so do not expect each school system to function without hesitation in the administration of the teacher aide program. The program growth rate has been increasing at a very rapid pace with eighty per cent of the teacher aide programs not in operation less than 10 years old. Conflicts and injustices in basic personnel policies involving employment, deployment, and implementation of aides will easily crop up in new, untried programs. However, time and experience will solve most problems.

If at first you are not allowed to attend staff meetings, re-member that time, experience and perseverance will lead to awareness on the part of the professional staff as to you as a source and an excellent, experienced contributor.

Will I, as a Teacher Aide, Have a Voice in Educational Policy-Making?

When faced with this question in a state wide survey taken in the State of Michigan, of 2,992 teachers and administrators, a scant 458 were in favor of allowing teacher aides a voice in educational policy-making, while 2,196 were opposed and 338 expressed no opinion.

To a high degree, this depends on the rank and status of the teacher aide in the school and the individual classroom in which the aide is employed.

If the schools dedicate themselves to the conceptual philosophy that every child is to receive a first-rate educational experience, our schools must be willing to listen with an attentive ear to all voices. Educators must realize that having a voice and an opportunity to speak is not in itself a mandate for action.

Innovation and dynamism will be found in a meaningful learning system only when the professional educators view themselves as learners along with the non-professionals and the students. Professionals must encourage and inculcate new approaches to staff and curricular development whenever possible for any voice that can offer new awareness or prospects of a new dimension to any topic or problem should be encouraged. No avenue of educational information should be left unexplored.

In the past teacher training institutions have failed to present the teacher aide concept in a realistic and meaningful manner, conditioning teacher to the belief that teachers are and should be the sole innovators and expediters of all things relating to the teaching and well-being of students entrusted to their care.

Two new concepts which bring added demands to the teacher are the idea that student development is increased and improved with additional adult attention and the idea that preventive educational measures are preferred to relying on remedial education.

Will I be Expected to Join a Professional or Sub-Professional Union Group?

It is human nature to belong to some group and the idea of organizing is an inherent quality in all groups bound by even a remote commonality. With this in mind, the question is where do you, as a teacher aide, best fit into the educational system—at the non-professional, semi-professional or professional level?

Contemporary educational thought favors a semi-professional organization for teacher aides. However, current administrators feel that teacher aides should be classified either non-professional or professional. They feel that two bargaining units are enough without the creation of a third. Actually, many administrators would like to see teacher aides remain strictly an hourly salaried group working on a contractual basis without any tangible connection to the schools over and above the hourly wage rate.

The current trend toward rapid implementation of teacher aides in the classroom yields programs ranging from the informal, nondescriptive to the formal, highly structured. Investigation indicated that semi-professional or associate memberships are being offered to teacher aides who have been required to undergo at least one year of post-high school training.

The type of membership you will be offered or required to accept will depend upon those available in your school district and the manner in which the aide program is viewed by the administration and the local education association.

CHAPTER VII

WHAT CONDITIONS CAN I EXPECT
IN THE CLASSROOM?

The law of life should not be the competition of acquisitiveness, but cooperation, the good of each contributing to the good of all.

Jawaharlal Nehru: Credo; circulated to friends; reprinted in the *New York Times* magazine, September 7, 1958.

What Conditions Can I Expect in the Classroom?

How Will I be Assigned to a Teacher?

There is no one, universal method for the assignment of teacher aides. To a great extent this depends entirely upon the school district in which you will be working.

Although a majority of the teachers desire teacher aides, aides should not be arbitrarily assigned. The assignment of an aide to a teacher should be to support the teacher and to be effective, the teacher must feel that she is being supported rather than having her position threatened. One reason that some teachers do not want an aide is because the professional feels the aide may usurp her power. A delicate balance must be struck which enables the aide to feel as if she is making a worthwhile contribution but also does not make the teacher feel she is losing her authority in the classroom. You can help the teacher adjust to your presence by assisting her rather than taking over her duties.

Ideally you will be assigned on a yearly basis. It is not fair to the teacher or to the aide to be forced to continually readjust to new superiors or new assistants. A long-term situation is conducive to mutual, confident, secure relationships between teacher and aide.

Realistically, it would be best to have the teacher choose her own aide as well as having you, the aide, choose your supervising teacher. The importance of a teacher-teacher aide team bond cannot be overemphasized. The success of a teacher aide program lies in the confidence and trust between the teacher and her aide.

Who Will be my Supervisor?

The state in which you will be a teacher aide will either have or will eventually have guidelines of legally sanctioned or certified practices for teacher aides. The local education association should have determined general guidelines and policies for the employment and deployment of aides in with the state's policies.

Within this framework the teacher should assign your responsibilities and tasks in a manner that will allow her to better teach the pupils.

Assuming that the teacher is your supervisor and you are her assistant, you should be directly responsible to that teacher— and to her only. It should be your supervising teacher's responsibility to plan the classroom activities and to fit you in where you will be of most benefit to her and the students.

School systems employ many methods of dealing with teacher aides. Ideally, as a teacher aide you should be responsible to only one person. This person should take an active role in your employment, deployment and career development. As an aide, you should not be forced into serving more than one supervisor unless your aide position is one that predicates working with several groups during the week. In this case you should still have one supervisor to whom you are to report and to whom you are to be held accountable for your actions.

As an Aide, how do I Develop a Working Relationship With my Supervising Teacher?

First, get acquainted with your supervising teacher. Relate information to your supervising teacher about yourself and your work experience which you feel may have some bearing on the performance of your duties.

Inquire about the teacher's previous experience. From this you may be able to determine areas in which the teacher may especially need your help. If the teacher is new to the area, you can acquaint her to school policies, traditions and customs.

Communication and cooperation between teacher and teacher aide are the two most pertinent factors leading to a successful aide program. Privately discuss things you do not understand or would like to have clarified.

You have been selected for the aide position because you have certain qualities desirable for the classroom. Try to do as much as you can to assist the teacher but do not set out to prove a point! When the teacher assigns you your duties—accept them cheerfully. Remember that she is the supervisor and you are the assistant.

What if I Don't get Along With my Supervising Teacher?

Ideally you should not be assigned to a specific teacher until you have met each other at least once and have shown some sign of amicability. You and teacher are not expected to become fast friends, but out-right animosity will not be expected either and it cannot be tolerated.

If friction develops within the course of the school year, you should discuss the problem with your supervising teacher first.

If you and your supervising teacher are still not able to meet on a common ground, you should speak to one of the supervisors of the program.

Don't complain to one of your co-workers—speak to someone who can take contructive steps to eliminate the problem. Try the constructive approach first and always, for backbiting will only cause greater friction.

To prevent personality problems in assignment of aides to teachers, many schools have informal coffee hours which give the potential aides and teachers an opportunity to meet on neutral ground and discuss issues relevant to teaching and teacher aide concepts. Teachers are then better able to judge and request a particular aide.

Most teachers who are involved in the selection process will put forth extra effort in helping their assigned aides adjust, for the ease of adjustment is a direct reflection of the supervising teacher's managerial and judgment ability, and teachers are anxious to vindicate their judgment ability and will make a special effort to see that the teacher of their selection makes a satisfactory and successful adjustment.

What Should I do With Problem Students Whom I Cannot Handle?

When you enter the school, and moreso the classroom, you are there for business and in order to attend to your business effectively you must conduct yourself in a professional manner. In your position as a professional aide you must set and maintain a professional distance from your students even though you must also develop rapport.

If you do not maintain professional distance, you will become a peer to the students and with this status the students may attempt to incorporate you into their social structure and you may not be placed in the leader's position. Once you lose your leadership, you have also lost your control.

Even with professional distance and hence, the attention of the majority of the students, you may have a problem with one or a few particular students. If a problem does occur, mention it to your supervising teacher and ask her help. If the teacher also has problems with these students, she will probably refer the students to the principal.

Do not take every display of undesirable behavior as being directed at you, personally. Many times students will have problems at home, or problems adjusting to the social life at school and when they "act up" it is because they are not able to cope with their problems. However, if a real problem does occur, ask your supervising teacher for assistance.

What About Teacher Aide Professionalism?

As an aide you will have access to privileged professional information. It is very important, to the teacher aide profession and to you personally, that you handle this information with the utmost prudence and care, always keeping the information confidential.

As an aide you must realize that you are identified with school service and the teaching profession, and that you must assume the responsibilities of your new role. You are required to adopt a standard of behavior commensurate with your position, one that is worthy of respect for yourself from the teachers, the students and the community.

Careless handling of information cannot be tolerated and is likely to bring reprimand to those concerned, for your actions can easily affect the entire school personnel structure from supervising teacher to school board president by the misuse of a bit of seemingly inconsequential information. When in doubt as to how to handle a certain piece of information, keep it confidential until you discuss it with your supervising teacher.

What Effect Will the Increased Introduction of Teacher Aides into the Classrooms Have on the Teaching Profession?

The planned and effective use of teacher aides in the classroom could prove to be one of the most significant advances in education. As teachers learn to use their newly released time from essential but inconsequential chores, their professional lives will take on a new perspective. Teachers will be able to devote more time to teaching while assuming a more professional role. New organizational structuring and planning will evolve from national to local levels as teacher involvement increases with new roles developing for both teachers and teacher aides.

The successful implementation of a teacher aide program will cause ramifications which will affect every segment of the present educational structure. Teacher training institutions will need to take into account, make allowances and preparations for this growing personnel dimension in education. It is possible that aide-intern service may become a regular part of teacher preparations.

The experience a new teacher gains from her internship as an aide will help her to better utilize the aide she is assigned. The internship will also give her experience that will enable her to be a better teacher.

Aide internship would also force colleges and schools to work together more closely in matters of planning, staffing and evaluation of teacher and teacher aide training curricula.

Will I as a Teacher Aide in the Classroom Make the Teacher Less Aware of Student Needs?

Ideally, in your capacity as a teacher aide, you will serve as an additional and active resource in keeping the teacher conscious of student needs. Your presence should give the teacher the advantage of another adult observer who will give the teacher insight, objective observations, and suggestions— when asked for.

Neglect of student needs could occur, but only if the teacher allows it to happen. There is no safeguard against this happening with or without an aide in the classroom, for the success or failure of any classroom endeavor rests largely upon the leadership of the teacher. It is the teacher's professional responsibility to remain alert and attentive to the student's needs. You are there to help her only, not to do her job.

Am I Being Hired Primarily as a Means of Increasing Classroom Enrollment?

No, the primary aim in hiring you, as a teacher aide, is to increase or enhance quality education.

A sample of teachers was asked whether they thought they would be more effective teaching classes of 25 to 30 and taking care of the non-instructional duties themselves, or teaching classes of 40 to 50 with a full-time aide to assist with non-teaching duties. Five in six teachers answered that they believed they would be more effective teaching the smaller group and taking care of all non-teaching duties.

Most teachers agree that any aide plan which offers any promise of relieving the overburdened teachers from non-educational or non-classroom duties will be embraced by the teacher with a normal classload, but not by that teacher who will be faced with a load increase. The aim in employing teacher aides is not to justify a heavier classload but to enhance the educational benefits of a normal class size.

What is to Prevent me From Being Used as a "Cheap Teacher?"

It is conceivable that violations in the implementation of teacher aides in the classroom instead of qualified teachers will be found occasionally.

Initially the function of all auxiliary personnel in a school system should be determined and given official approval by the appropriate agencies. The State Department of Education should determine the functional boundaries for teacher aides requiring only local jurisdictional approval and specific boundaries for aide areas requiring state approval.

Basic safeguarding on the part of the local education association could easily serve as the deterrent and the policy agency for all auxiliary personnel operations.

Basically, it is the responsibility of your supervising teacher to see that you are used only in a legitimate capacity. The local educational organization should also have as one of its primary responsibilities the policing of teacher aides to insure that you as an aide are not being exploited beyond your specified, sanctioned, or certified capacity.

If you feel that you are being exploited or you view injustices within the program, you should first talk with your supervising teacher and ask for a clarification of the ground rules. If you still feel there are injustices within the program, follow proper procedure and ask to be allowed to speak with the pertinent administrative source.

Would I, as an Aide, be Allowed to Teach?

As a teacher aide you will not be allowed to teach formally as you may initially conceive teaching, but you will help the teacher to teach.

"The distinguishing characteristic of the qualified teacher is her ability to analyze the instructional needs of her students and to prescribe the elements of formal schooling that will best meet those needs. In this view, it is altogether proper for the teacher aide to be more than a clerical aide. The usefulness of the teacher aide should be restricted only by her own personal limitations in whatever duties she may be assigned by the regular classroom teacher." [1]

With this in mind it is possible to have the teacher aide perform such tasks that were previously restricted to performance by the teacher. The teacher aide could then drill children on arithmetic tables, spelling words and reading drills. The aide could also correct assignment papers, listen to children read and help either individuals or small groups with specific problem areas.

As an aide you can also expect to supervise playground or rainy-day indoor activities and in the event of class trips, help the teacher make arrangements for the trip, and help supervise the group on the trip.

Will I be Allowed to View Student Records?

If in the performance of your duties it becomes necessary for you to review a student's cumulative record, you should be allowed to do so. All teacher aides, regardless of their employment capacity, will come into contact with certain confidential information concerning either a student or the school.

Before being allowed to view or being given access to confidential information, you should be given instruction as to its proper

---

[1] Thorwald Esbensen, "Should Teacher Aides Be More Than Clerks?" *Phi Delta Kappan* 47: 237: January, 1966.

use and the consequences involved in instances of its misuse. It is imperative that you, as an aide, are aware of the ramifications involved in your actions and the necessity of treating all confidential information with a high degree of professional standards.

Teacher aides, when and where the necessity arises in the performance of their duties, should be allowed access to all the pertinent confidential information required. Your assigned aide duties should specify the type and amount of personal and confidential information to be released. In fact, it should be the responsibility of the supervising teacher to see that her assigned aide is provided with all the pertinent information needed to carry out her assigned task proficiently.

Each teacher aide, at least after her initial employment meeting, should without any doubt know that a breach of confidential ethics will not be tolerated. To maintain high moral and ethical teaching standards, procedures for discipline need to be established, clarified and enforced.

As an Aide, Just What Will my Responsibilities be?

As an aide your primary function and responsibility is to increase the effectiveness of the teacher in the classroom. Theoretically, a teacher should be able to arrange the formal learning environment of her classroom in such a manner as to meet the goals of instruction. Essentially the distinguishing factor of a competent teacher is the capability of making certain kinds of decisions. [2]

Instructional material, such as texts and audio-visual aids, is usually commercially prepared and distributed. The materials

---

[2]   *Ibid.*

are available but it is the teacher who decides which are to be used and how, when and where they are to be used.

As an aide you can expect to do anything the teacher asks you to do in assisting her with the preparation, presentation and summation of classroom activity.

You should not be asked to formally evaluate a student's progress but under the teacher's direction you may be requested to test him and record his progress.

You may not be allowed to teach children to read but you should be able to read to children and listen patiently while they read to you.

You may not be able to teach an art class, but you should be able to assemble the necessary materials and assist where necessary. If you have artistic talents you should be allowed to instruct an art class, make comments, assist students and give praise.

In your position as an aide, you are capable and should be allowed and expected to be more than a clerk and a book-keeper. Your usefulness should be limited only by your capabilities and creativity, ingenuity and managerial skills of your supervising teacher.

As a Certified Aide, Will I be Able to Serve as a Substitute Teacher?

In all likelihood, if the need arises you will be called on to serve as a substitute teacher.

Generally educators agree that substitute teachers are often strictly a holding action. As a group, substitute teachers are the least capable of coping with varying classroom climates. It is unrealistic to believe that substitute teachers are able to bring any more than a facsimile of course continuity and progress to the classroom.

In the absence of the teacher, you as a certified aide would serve as the best substitute because:

1) You are acquainted with the students

2) You are a part of and a participant in the day-to-day developments of your assigned classroom

3) You are aware of the teacher's aims and objectives

4) Your familiarity with the classroom will enable you to eliminate the basic confusion and disorder connected with substitute teachers

5) You are familiar with school and classroom routines and procedures

As a Certified Aide Serving as a Substitute Teacher, how Will I be Supervised?

In order to prevent both you and the teachers from being exploited, basic rules must be set and rigidly adhered to. The following regulations prevail in governing the service of certified aides as substitute teachers.

1) Certified aides must have state certification

2) As a certified aide you will be permitted to teach only in classes in which you are regularly employed

3) You must have the recommendation of your supervising teacher as to your capabilities and responsibility

4) You will be permitted to serve only in cases where the teacher's absence is caused by illness or days covered by the teacher's professional absence days

5) You will be limited to approximately 24 teaching days per year, based on the possibility of substituting for two teachers for whom the aide may regularly assist,

allowing for 10 sick days and two professional leave days per year per teacher

6) You must have the sanction of the local education association for this type of substitute teaching

What is the Teacher Aide Concept in Relation to Staff Development?

Try as they may, good teachers are invariably forced to neglect student needs because of the non-instructional non-student demands of the bureaucratized institution of education. Time that a teacher should and would spend on instructional and educative processes is consumed with the maintenance of records, attendance at meetings and public relations with parents and the community.

If every school-age child is to receive the best education possible, the teachers must be given the opportunity to use their education, training and abilities to the maximum. To enable a teacher to do this she must be provided with the element of time—time during which the students are in school. Staff development, in the nature of teacher aides, gives the teacher more time to do the job she is trained to do and is employed to do—to teach.

The one-adult classroom is destined to pass out of existence as the recognition that teaching is a team effort and aides are a vital part of that team comes of age. A team program can develop better educational programs and methods by cooperation of experts and generalists.

The cooperative team teaching staff is supported by educational developments yielding the beliefs that: [3]

---

[3] Roy A. Edelfelt, "The Teacher And His Staff," Virginia Journal of Education, April, 1967, pp. 12-13.

1) a variety of people and talents are needed to staff schools adequately.

2) prospective teachers and in-service teachers at various stages of professional development can contribute in different ways to school programs.

3) the role of the teacher should depend on competence, experience, attitude and desire.

4) responsibility, competence, status and reward should be related, that is, a teacher should have one of these qualities of the degree to which he has the others.

5) there should be a visible career pattern in the teaching profession which makes remaining in the classroom rewarding to those who want to stay in teaching.

6) a career in teaching should offer enough variety in assignment to provide stimulation and new experiences throughout a teacher's tenure.

7) there should be more than one adult working with a group of youngsters so as to provide professional stimulation, perspective and attention to each student.

8) teacher aides can perform paraprofessional tasks under the supervision of a certified teacher.

9) implementation of the staff program would decrease the student-adult ratio rather than increase it.

Knowledgeable educators realize that if teacher aides are to become an integral part of the educational process, the teacher aide concept must be given structure and order in theory and practice. They are rapidly acknowledging the need for and merit of teacher aides and are taking the stand that contemporary staff development is not a complete process if it fails to understand and take into account concepts and practices involving teacher aides.

How can I, as a Teacher Aide, Become a Part of an Efficient, Productive Classroom Routine?

You can be best assimilated into the educational program through proper planning and assignment. Ideally, any conflicting individual differences held either by the teacher or you as an aide should be recognized and resolved before you and teacher are faced with the initial classroom experience.

The educational objectives and operational procedures should be planned in accordance with the most feasible and greatest combined strength of the teacher and you, her aide.

When you, as a third entity, enter the classroom situation, many new psychological set relationships develop between the teacher, you and the students. The teacher-student relationship is inevitably altered and unless a great deal of time is spent on the many ramifications inherent in this "parlaying triangle" there will be more problems than from all other problem areas combined.

In-service training should satisfy most of your operational needs and resolve many of your problems. However, actual task orientation and indoctrination into the multi-faceted educational system will primarily be the task of your supervising teacher.

It is incumbent upon your supervising teacher to discover and bring out any special talents you may have, utilizing them wisely and proficiently. It should also be incumbent upon your supervising teacher to have regularly scheduled conferences devoted to guiding you to your fullest potential.

Experienced administrators agree that where the direction and work assignments of the aide are concerned there should be only one supervisor: the teacher. The success or failure of any school's endeavor rests largely with the classroom teacher and there is no substitute for a good one.

It is important for the students to understand the educational concept of the teacher aide. They must realize that the teacher is the educational team leader and not the "boss." The teacher who is cognizant of the fact that leadership is not command will be most successful.

It is your supervising teacher's responsibility to set the tone of your teacher-teacher aide relationship and to do so effectively, the teacher must have the full authority to make and be responsible for all classroom decisions.

The degree of responsibility assigned to you as an aide is dependent upon your interaction with your supervising teacher with both of you operating within a given structure and responding to the specific needs of the students in that particular classroom.

Planning between you as a teacher aide and your supervising teacher that would promote interaction with the students might include: [4]

1. Helping the aide develop an understanding of a healthy relationship between herself, the teacher and the students.

2. Clarifying the discipline role of the aide.

3. Helping the aide recognize the need to allow children to make errors and approach tasks carefully.

4. Sharing of information between teacher and teacher aide that will help in dealing with the students.

5. Helping the aide become open-minded and objective.

---

[4] Clarence Lacny, Utilizing Teacher Aides in the Jackson, Michigan, Public Schools, "A Dual Opportunity," Jackson Public Schools, 1970.

6. Helping the aide learn how she can contribute to communications between:

   a. teacher-pupil
   b. pupil-teacher
   c. pupil-pupil

7. Helping you, as an aide develop a realistic viewpoint about children.

8. Giving you, as an aide, a clear assignment of your duties and responsibilities as they are developed.

9. Developing a team attitude.

How do the Teacher and I Employ the Teacher-Teacher Aide Team Concept?

When you assume the teacher aide role, you, in some manner, become a part of an instructional team which functions as an extension of the master teacher. The teacher is the team supervisor and as such she has the responsibility of coordinating the educational growth of the whole child.

When working in the aide capacity, you must remember that, even though you are making a valuable contribution to the educational process, you have a subordinate role. You must be flexible enough to do whatever the teacher asks.

You may assume tasks without the teacher dictating your every move, but you should realize the limits of your authority and not usurp the professional power of the teacher. The key to a successful teacher-teacher aide relationship is free communication, flexibility of tasks and trust. The attitude of an effective team approach is:

"Which of us can best perform this task in a way that will give the most help to the greatest number of pupils?"

CHAPTER VIII

WHAT ARE THE VARIOUS AIDE CATEGORIES AND THEIR RESPONSIBILITIES?

As the curriculum leader moves from school to school and from group to group within the school system's organization, different situational ingredients operate. According to the situational theory, no single status leader can hope to perform with extreme initiative in all the groups with which he meets, and still perform effectively in many of them. In this sense, the significance of emergent leadership and release of leadership potential in others is forced upon him.

Ronald C. Doll, *Curriculum Improvement: Decision-Making and Process* (Boston: Allyn and Bacon, Inc., 1964), p. 162.

What are the Various Aide Categories and Their Responsibilities?

What are the Different Teacher Aide Classifications? — "The Brighton Concept"

Generally, there are eight distinct Teacher Aide Classifications:

Student Aides
Mother Aides
Father Aides
Volunteer Aides
Special Aides
Practical Aides
Certified Aides
Reader-Grader Aides

Within each aide category, the aide performs specific functions within a structural framework. No school would need or be expected to use all eight aide classifications, but there is no reason why they could not if they so desired.

The classification of aides should either be based on a certification system or a sanctioning system. Basic requirements of each aide classification should be defined by the State Department of Education or its equivalent in each state.

Superintendents usually delegate authority to sub-administrators or the local educational association for implementation and operation of the aide program. The local educational association is usually given a strong consultive, if not active administrative role in the employment and deployment of teacher aides.

What are Student Aides?

A student aide is any elementary or secondary student who is used in either a paid or voluntary capacity to help teachers in any of their duties either within or without the school.

You, as a student aide, can perform the following duties:

1) Maintain weight and measurement charts of other students

2) Help the teacher conduct students to various school activities

3) Arrange displays of student work

4) Write lesson assignment and teachers instructions on the chalkboard

5) Put the daily schedule on the chalkboard

6) Supervise a small group while the teacher is busy with other students

7) Maintain library records

8) Supervise or referee educational and recreational games

9) Read or tell stories to the class

10) Conduct individual students to appointments within the building

11) Serve as host or hostess at parent-teacher conferences

12) Help individual children with motor coordination activities

13) Help individual children identify and form letters and numbers

14) Make name tags

15) Duplicate instructional materials for the teacher

16) Prepare drill materials

17) File materials

18) Prepare visual aids

19) Gather materials and books for the teacher and the class

20) Listen to children read

21) Distribute and collect specific lesson materials

22) Prepare, set-up, operate and return instructional materials and equipment

23) Prepare materials for art, science and special projects

24) Construct various charts

25) Help with special education and home projects

26) Check to see that children understand the teacher's directions

27) Maintain representative work folders for each student

28) Help supervise lunchroom

29) Assist with recess and preparing children to go home

30) Run errands for the teacher

31) Decorate the classroom and bulletin boards for various holidays and seasons

32) Collect milk, lunch, picture and trip monies

33) Assist the teacher on field trips

34) Check pupils for weather dress and aid with dressing difficulties

35) Monitor the halls

36) Monitor school buses on trips to and from school and on school trips

37) Maintain and check-out recreational and special equipment

38) Serve as a safety officer

39) Help direct students during fire and tornado drills

40) Help slow students review letter, number and word identification

41) Assist with the preparation and service of food

42) Assist with the physical needs of children such as going to the washroom and washing up, etc.

43) Write for free and inexpensive materials the teacher has requested

44) Help take care of classroom pets and plants

45) File and catalogue material

46) Play piano or other musical instruments

47) Distribute materials and help students locate specific materials.

This list is not exclusive, nor is it meant to serve as a permissive or restrictive guide for any student aide program. It is your supervising teacher's prerogative to add or subtract basic housekeeping, bookkeeping and storekeeping duties according to her view of the situational classroom needs.

As a student aide, you should be encouraged to participate in as many classroom activities as possible. In the classroom situation, you are not only helping the teacher do her job more effectively, you are also in a position to learn by doing and thus gain insight and experience in the teaching profession.

What are Mother Aides?

Mother aides are room mothers who volunteer to assist the teacher with various classroom activities. Generally, mother aides are not assigned regularly scheduled classroom duties, but they do assist the teacher in planning, preparing and carrying out various sporadically spaced classroom functions.

As a Mother Aide, What Duties can I Expect to Perform?

The mother aide classification does not take into account factors of advanced training or special talent. If you have advanced or special training and wish to serve in the capacity, you may prefer another aide category.

Generally, as a mother aide you can expect to:

1) Supervise the loading and unloading of school buses.

2) Serve as a school bus driver.

3) Serve as a school bus driver for field trips.

4) Conduct sick students either home or to a doctor.

5) Chaperone school activities.

91

6) Supervise the lunchroom and halls during the noon hour.

7) Plan holiday parties and programs.

8) Assist with student health care.

9) Manage the room library and keep it stocked with material from outside sources.

10) Supervise milk and lunch programs.

11) Inventory and account for non-consumable goods.

12) Serve as confidant to both students and teacher.

These duties are guidelines, not limits, or mother aide duties. The amount of time that you elect to spend in the classroom will, to a degree, dictate your range of duties. As you become familiar with classroom duties, both you and the teacher may want to increase your range of duties.

What Type and how Much In-Service Training Should Mother Aides Have?

Your training for the mother aide role is likely to be in the form of an indoctrination session and at least one follow-up session. These sessions should highlight the needs and responsibilities of your new role. Not only are these sessions to acquaint you with your new duties and responsibilities, but they are to give you greater exposure and new awareness of the complex educational system.

Before any specific task, the supervising teacher will probably call or meet with you to explain just exactly what your function will be. Do not hesitate to ask her questions. If you know what is expected of you, both you and your supervising teacher will be happier because you will be able to perform your assigned tasks without hesitation.

What are Father Aides?

Father aides, like mother aides, are room fathers who volunteer to give varying amounts of their time to assist with classroom connected activities. The implementation of father aides in the classroom may be the first step away from the traditional matriarchal domination of teacher aides while helping to fill the void created by a lack of adult masculine influence in contemporary schools.

The father aide concept is based on the theory that boys and girls benefit immeasurably from exposure to male patterning figures. Contemporary research has shown that youths can develop a wholesome role identification if exposed to more men in the learning situation. Because of the changing occupational structure, more men are having more free time during the school day. When fathers are available, it is very important for them to be in the classroom during the school day.

Father aides need not be highly trained or specialized. Desirable characteristics for father aides are imagination, creativity, inspirational attitudes, friendly demeanor, patience, tolerance, ability to relate to children, an easily identifiable masculine attitude and, above all a sincere desire to work with children.

As a Father Aide, What Type and how Much In-Service Training Should I Expect to Undergo?

As a father aide, you will probably be required to attend at least one indoctrination and one follow-up session. The training session is to acquaint you with the duties and responsibilities of a father aide, while the follow-up sessions are as much a learning device for school administrators as they are for you.

Since father aides are a relatively new concept, administrators will eagerly await reports of your reception in the classroom by teachers, other aides and more particularly, the children's response and reaction to your presence in the learning environment.

Your formal training session will be primarily an indoctrination session with heavy emphasis on school policy and procedures. As you proceed with the classroom routine, your supervising teacher will tell you what to do and how to do it. As you become familiar with the class and the teacher, you will assume duties without being expressly directed by the teacher. At this point, you must be careful not to overstep your bounds and usurp the teacher's territorial rights. When in doubt, ask.

As a Father Aide, What Duties can I Expect to Perform?

Like the mother aide category, the father aide category does not take into consideration advanced training or special talents. If you have advanced training or special talents, you may prefer another aide category with duties commensurate to your training and talent.

Generally, as a father aide, you should be able to perform all duties listed for student aides in addition to those listed for mother aides.

Duties which are specifically geared to the father aide category are:

1) Helping students in construction activities such as play props, aquariums, terrariums, etc.

2) Assisting with camping trips, nature hikes, picnics.

3) Teaching folklore, nature appreciation.

4) Helping a teacher "reach" a problem student, particularly those from fatherless homes.

5) Giving students a strong, stable masculine image.

In this modern world where it is getting harder to differentiate the mothers from the fathers, growing children have a difficult time defining their roles without a proper masculine influence. Your masculine character is needed in the classroom, to help the teacher, but moreso to help guide the students.

What are Volunteer Teacher Aides?

A volunteer teacher aide is any person who is engaged by a school system to voluntarily devote time to the performance of various duties, either within or without the classroom as agreed upon by legally responsible, educational supervisory personnel. Because the volunteer aide program is the offering of innumerable free services to schools by dedicated individuals, the volunteer aid category is open-ended to allow individuals in all capacities and availability statuses to volunteer their services.

Volunteer aides spend as much or as little time in the classroom as is mutually convenient for both the aide and the school.

The duties a volunteer aide can perform are limited only by her skill and educational background and the teacher's ingenuity in utilizing the aide. Volunteer aides have a greater immediate need and deployment potential than any other aide category because of the flexibility of their services and hours.

The volunteer aide can serve one specific teacher or she may serve many teachers in the same school or she may "float" from school to school depending on the need for her services.

As a Volunteer Aide, What Kind of Training Will I Have?

Like the preceding aide categories, your formal training will probably consist of an indoctrination session and a follow-up session. Basically, the indoctrination session is to acquaint you with school policies and procedures and the follow-up session is to give you a chance to speak up about problems, difficult situations and to discuss new experiences.

Because volunteer aides' hours and services are so irregular and varied, your on-the-job training will consist mainly of teacher instructions before each task assignment.

As a Volunteer Aide, What Duties can I Expect to Perform?

Generally, as a volunteer aide, you will perform miscellaneous housekeeping functions, provide receptionist and guide services for visitors, perform various clerical duties and act as a resource person. You may work in the library, cafeteria, school clinic, gymnasium, special services area or the classroom.

You may be called in only once during the school year or once a week or you may know of a specific need and volunteer your services for that specific need on a scheduled basis.

If you volunteer to help the school nurse, you may come in only when she is in attendance or you may come in every day or once a week to keep the clinic and supplies in good order.

If you provide receptionist and guide services, you may be in school during the school day, every day or once a week, or you may volunteer to serve during open houses only.

The duties you can perform as a volunteer aide are limited only by your imagination, your ambitions, your abilities and the school's needs.

What are Special Aides?

The special aide classification is designed to give credence and order to the classification of persons who bring specialized enrichment to the regular school program.

As far as qualifications are concerned, special aides could be classified in any of the aide categories. As the title implies, you are special for you perform a specific or unique function. Your duties are confined to your specific talent area and your services are generally available to more than one teacher.

This type of aide employment and implementation will not generally be dependent upon the amount of attained formal educational training. Special aides are "special" for they perform specialized and unique functions within and without the school system under the direct supervision of the school administrators. Aides of this categorical type may be either paid or volunteer, student or adult.

As a Special Aide, What Type of and how Much In-Service Training Will I Have?

To a great degree this will depend on which special aide category you choose. All special aides will be required to have an indoctrination session concerning school policies and procedures. Further sessions will deal with the specific duties of each aide category. These sessions will vary in length and complexity according to the nature of the aide category and assigned placement.

What Specific Duties can a Special Education Aide Perform?

As an aide in a special education classroom, you can help the teacher to better meet the needs of these special students by making observations and reporting to the teacher in charge. You may also administer routine tests and report the results to the teacher or chart each student's progress for the teacher's review. You may maintain attendance records; maintain and file general organizational records; prepare, distribute and maintain classroom materials and equipment.

Although it is your supervising teacher's responsibility to prepare the lesson plan, you may take an active part in presenting a part of the plan to the students.

As an aide in a special education classroom, you are a particular asset, for you double the adult-pupil contact and provide for double adult observation and perception of the students and their individual problems. In this manner you perform your primary task, that of extending the human emotional responsitivity of the professional person. '

In performing this function you are oriented toward three objectives:

1) Helping handicapped children attain their highest achievement level by concentrating on what the student can do well and then praising him for it. Your introduction into the classroom will allow more personal adult contact for the student by both the teacher and the aide which will give the student the increased attention he needs to motivate and encourage him.

2) Helping handicapped children to build a better self-concept. Handicapped children are faced not only with coping with their limitations but also the complications of non-sympathetic and overly-sympathetic people in the outside world. Handicapped children need help in accepting and valuing themselves.

3) Helping the handicapped child develop the curiosity which is a sign of the person who has developed enough self-confidence to leave his sheltered, sure surroundings and explore. As an aide in the classroom, you can give a handicapped child the encouragement to develop

' Field testing and demonstration of on the job training of paraprofessionals to serve as members of teams operating type A classrooms for mentally handicapped, accompanied by in-service training of teachers serving on teams, Branch County Intermediate School Offices, 66 South Monroe Street, Coldwater, Michigan, p. 19.

interpersonal relationships and more important, you can be a party to one of these initial relationships that help him to develop his self-confidence.

What are Practical Aides?

A practical aide is any person who, in the opinion of the aide selection committee has qualities conducive to the overall betterment of the educational program.

Most often as a practical aide your duties will be confined to either very narrow specialties or the more menial and clerical duties.

As a Practical Aide, What Type and how Much Training Should I Have?

Generally, for employment in the practical aide category, you will be required to have a high school diploma or its equivalent.

Prior to the fall opening of school, you may be required to spend one full week (40 hours) in basic orientation and training. This experience will give you a general over-view of the school, its policies and procedures and your general job assignment.

During the school year, you may be required to attend one hour sessions per school week. These sessions will probably be allotted to planned training orientation to new procedures and consultation. At these sessions you will be encouraged to share your experiences and discuss any problems that may have arisen.

As a Practical Aide, What Duties can I Expect to Perform?

As a practical aide you should be able to perform all the functions required of the student, mother and father aides.

This overlap is necessary and should be expected for in many schools there will not be student, mother or father aides and you may be requested to perform some of their tasks.

As a practical aide, particularly, you will be expected to be able to perform the following functions:

1) Give extra help to students who do not understand assignments

2) Assist students with difficult information and pertinent information on missed assignments and make-up work

3) Record data on cumulative records

4) Correct and grade assignment papers, workbooks and reports and projects

5) Correct objective tests

6) Score and profile achievement and diagnostic tests

7) Serve as a laboratory assistant

8) Serve as an instructional and project demonstrator

9) Conduct reading and spelling groups

10) Serve as a proctor

11) Average academic marks

12) Complete school and county reports

13) Supervise the class when the teacher must leave

14) Keep attendance records

15) Telephone parents on routine matters such as verifying notes for requests to leave school early and to check on student absences

16) Help prepare school newspaper materials

17) Enter grades into teacher's record book

18) Supervise club meetings

19) Supervise indoor games on rainy days

20) Prepare introductions to audio-visual materials to provide students with background in either using or viewing them

21) Escort injured or sick students, who have no telephone or transportation, home

22) Escort an injured or sick child to a doctor or hospital

23) Conduct tutorials with individuals or small groups

24) Decorate the classroom or auditorium for special occasions

These limits are not a restriction or permissive guide in your range of duties. Within your assigned school the administrator and your supervising teacher will decide on the limits of your duties.

What are Certified Aides?

A certified aide has at least one year of formalized post-high school training and is usually certified by the State Department of Education. This certification legally sanctions your performance of semi-instructional classroom activities, while under the direct supervision of a certified teacher.

As a Certified Aide, how Much and What Type of Training Will I be Required to Have?

In this aide category you will be required to have completed at least one year or 30 semester hours of post high school training. This training should be in educational areas deemed pertinent to the enhancement of a quality performance as a teacher aide.

101

You will serve at least one-year in internship as a practical aide or you will be required to show proof of equivalent experience.

As a newly certified aide you should be required to spend one week in orientation and training prior to the opening of school in the fall. During the school year you will probably be required to attend weekly in-service training sessions. These weekly sessions may be with the supervising teacher or in some other planned activity, either individual or group.

As a Certified Aide, What Duties can I Expect to Perform?

Because of your range of experience, you will be allowed, but not required, to perform all the duties which are required of student, mother, father and practical aides. Other duties that you should be able to perform are:

1) Leading the class or a group in simple comprehensive, skill, appreciation or drill exercises

2) Tutor individual students

3) Brief students on missed or misunderstood instructions

4) Preview and report on films and other audio-visual aids

5) Proofread and edit student copy for student newspapers

6) File correspondence and other reports in student records

7) Obtain special material for special class projects

8) Supervise various auxiliary school projects

9) Organize and supervise intramural activities and programs

10) Assist or direct skits and plays

11) Teach and emphasize good conduct and etiquette

12) Assist students with basic writing skills such as composition grammar, and punctuation

13) Arrange field trips, collect parental permission forms, insure correct scheduling, inform students of safety and dress regulations

14) Confer with teachers and/or students regarding specific behavior problems

15) Confer with teachers and/or the principal regarding specific students

16) Conduct routine classroom activities

17) Assist teachers with basic research problems

18) Assist the teacher in developing and organizing classroom material

19) Observe students and report exaggerated behavior, both positive and negative, to the teacher

20) Serve as a substitute teacher when the regular teacher is absent

21) Assist the teacher with class presentations

What are Reader and Grader Aides?

Reader and grader aides are utilized only in checking compositions for errors in capitalization, punctuation, spelling, sentence structure, word usage and basic theme organization. As a reader-grader aide, you may be asked to comment on the structure and means for improvement of the basic composition.

You can also expect to grade vocabulary tests, written drills, extra work, special projects and objective tests. Although all grade assignments must be the direct responsibility of the teacher, as a reader-grader aide, you may be asked to recommend letter grades for all paper content passing before you.

You may or may not have an assigned work station at the school for most of your work is flexible enough to fit almost any individual situation.

Generally speaking, for employment in the reader-grader aide category you will need a college degree. In hiring reader-grader aides, in most cases, heavy emphasis and preference will be given to those who have a major in English.

Aside from the education requirement, the screening process will probably include successful completion of a standardized language proficiency test, in addition to an oral interview dealing primarily with both the understanding of and cooperation with youth and skill development philosophies.

As a Reader-Grader Aide, What Type and how Much In-Service Training Will I Have to Have?

As a reader-grader aide you will probably be required to attend an orientation session to get acquainted with staff members and to orient yourself to your new duties, expectations and responsibilities.

You will probably be required to attend at least one follow-up session to cover any missed or misunderstood points of the initial orientation session and to discuss any questions that may arise after your initial job confrontation.

If you do not have an assigned station in the school, it is important that you be available and make occasional visits to the school while classes are in session, for the overall success of this type of teacher-teacher aide involvement is highly dependent upon harmonious work relationships and open communication channels.

It is your supervising teacher's responsibility to provide you with a standard set of evaluative and corrective marking symbols.

She should also inform you as to what type of errors to look for in each particular assignment.

Employment in this category requires and should demand planned periodical conference sessions between the supervising teacher and you, her reader-grader aide. It is all too easy for the students to be caught in a triangular situation if the aide program is not well-structured. In your capacity as a reader-grader aide, you should never be set-up as a "scape goat" for either the teacher or the students.

As a Reader-Grader Aide, What Duties can I Expect to Perform?

As a reader-grader aide you can expect to:

1) Make helpful and corrective notes on student's written work

2) Suggest ways in which the students may improve their work and recommend specific resource materials

3) Hold tutorial conferences with individual students

4) Recommend writing and outline techniques

5) Inform the teacher of student and course content deficiencies as evidenced by work on student papers

6) Express your views and personal observations regarding improvement of corrective markings or techniques to your supervising teacher

7) Conduct remedial classes and act as an outside resource person

8) Supervise student make-up assignments and extra-duty

9) Serve as a consultive resource person for the teacher

10) Conduct group indoctrination sessions on phases of writing and forms of expression.

Note: As a reader-grader aide it is very important to your personal adjustment on the job and the success of your employment experience that you are sure of the teacher's ground rules before performing any of the above functions. It is necessary that you and the teacher or teachers are in "operational agreement" before you attempt to carry out any third person activities.

What are the Various Aide Categories and What Duties Could be Expected in Each One?

Contemporary practices involving the use of special aides are as expansive as the educational curricula. A few of the more widely known and practiced special aide categories are:

Audio-Visual Technician

> Training for audio-visual technicians would include maintenance and operation of the audio-visual equipment. The audio-visual technician would inventory, store, maintain and operate audio-visual equipment.

Classroom Aide

> The classroom aide performs clerical, monitorial and teacher re-enforcement tasks under the direct supervision of the classroom teacher.

Counselor Aide

> Under the direction of the counselor, the aide performs clerical, monitorial and counseling re-enforcement tasks.

Lunchroom Aide

> According to school practices, the lunchroom aide supervises the lunchroom during lunch periods, maintains order, helps children when assistance is needed,

works with administrators and teachers to improve
procedures and supervises after-lunch playground or
special activities.

Community Aide

The community aide acts as a liaison person between
the school and the community to inform parents of school
and community services and to inform teachers of
community problems and special needs.

Hospitality Aide

The hospitality aide receives parents who visit the
school and, under the direction of the principal, conducts
the parents to a conference room. The aide may also
arrange for refreshments for teachers, parents and
students.

Departmental Aide

Working in a particular department, the aide will perform
designated departmental tasks such as record-keeping,
inventory, scoring objective tests and arranging for
materials on teachers' requests.

General School Aide

Not assigned to a single station, the general school
aide performs a variety of school duties as assigned by
the principal, assistant principal or designated teacher.
The aide may assist at doors and in halls, the office,
bookstore, library, clinic or classroom.

Library Aide

Under the supervision of the certificated librarian the
aide assists in the operation of the school library by

shelving, filing, clipping, circulation and book processing. The aide may help students locate books and reference materials.

Testing Service Aide

The testing service aide works with professional testers in schools or regional centers to arrange for, administer, check and record student test results.

Teacher-Clerical Aide

Serving an individual teacher, the teacher-clerical aide keeps the records for an individual teacher.

School Security Aide

Usually assigned by the principal, the school security aide is responsible for checking doors, corridors, lavatories, parking lots and for the banking of school receipts.

After-School Program Aide

Under the direction of a teacher, the after-school program aide supervises after-school activities.

Materials Resource Center Assistant
(Program Learning Lab Assistant)

This aide performs clerical, custodial and monitorial functions in a material resource center or program learning laboratory.

Special Talent Aide

This aide has special talents to assist in teaching art, music, and crafts.

Special Skills Aide

> This aide assists the teacher by having special skills in the areas of shop, homemaking or speaking a foreign language.

Crisis Center Aide (Opportunity Room)

> In the Opportunity Room, aides work with children who have problems adjusting in the regular classroom situation.

Playground (Recreational) Aide

> Playground aides work with teachers during the school day to assist with physical education activities.

Reading Improvement Aide

> In addition to reading stories and serving as a listener, the reading improvement aide assists the reading specialist with basic and remedial reading instruction in a single school or group of schools.

Special Education Aide

> The special education aide assists the special education teacher in implementing instruction and activities for individuals or groups of special education pupils.

Speech Correction Aide

> Working under the direction of the speech correctionist, the aide serves to provide increased correctional services for pupils with speech problems.

Attendance Officer Aide

> The attendance officer aide provides assistance in dealing with attendance problems and may make home calls whose purpose is delineated by the attendance officer.

Bus Attendant Aide

> At the beginning and end of the school day this aide supervises loading and unloading of school buses. The aide may ride the buses, particularly those buses transporting very young children. The aide may also help with field trip activities and supervision.

High School Theme Reader

> The theme reader reads and checks class themes for those aspects of writing indicated by the teacher.

Health Clinic Aide

> Under the direction of the school nurse or a visiting nurse, the clinic aide maintains the school clinic.

Laboratory Technician

> Under the direction of science and language teachers the laboratory technician sets up, maintains and operates equipment and prepares and distributes equipment to students.

Enrichment Opportunity Aide

> The enrichment opportunity aide provides general and additional in-depth tutorial or personalized assistance.

What are Subject or Area Specialist Aides?

Communities which are fortunate enough to have a person or persons with special talents or abilities and who is willing to share these talents or abilities with students should take advantage of the situation. The time that these people may be able to offer should be incorporated into a schedule that is flexible enough to benefit as many students as possible.

As such an aide you could "float" from class to class and school to school on a flexible schedule that would permit your availability to be interwoven with the students' needs and availabilities.

This floating method would allow many more students to benefit from your talent than is possible in the one-aide-to-a-classroom method. Serving in this particular aide category you could also be involved in extra curricular activities during the evening hours such as an informal club rather than a scheduled class. A strict schedule is not as important as is getting the aide and the students together.

As a subject or area specialist you will serve as a motivator rather than a supervisor. Your continued presence is not necessary for you will direct and guide students in areas in which the teacher is limited, rather than assume classroom duties.

What is a Counselor Aide?

In 1966 the American Personnel and Guidance Association adopted a statement of policy encouraging the use of supportive personnel for the school counselor. The A.P.G.A. took the position that appropriately prepared supportive personnel, under the supervision of the professional counselor, can contribute to meeting the school's needs by enhancing the work of the counselor. [2]

The assigned duties and functions of the counselor aide are quite different from those of other aides and must be dealt with accordingly. As a counselor aide you will perform only specific functions and only under the supervision of the counselor, while the counselor synthesizes and integrates the interrelated

---

[2] *Support Personnel for the Counselor: Their Technical and Non-Technical Roles and Preparation*, Personnel and Guidance Journal, April, 1967.

parts of the total range of services with and in behalf of the counselee.

Your duties as a counselor aide are divided into two groups: those of direct helping relationships and those of indirect helping relationships.[3] Direct helping relationships are those activities which relate to both individual and small-group interviewing functions which the counselor feels the aide may adequately perform. Direct helping relationships are those activities which relate to both individual and small-group interviewing functions which the professional counselor feels that you are capable of performing.

Indirect helping relationships are such as information gathering and processing, assisting with referrals, placement and follow-up procedures and program management. Clerical duties are included in this category but they should not be stressed. If the job description is mainly clerical, it may be better to have a secretary and give her some counselor aide training.

A good counselor aide training program should have at least four major phases: 1) screening and admission 2) pre-service orientation to the job 3) in-service preparation and 4) on-the-job training.

In order to perform your work skillfully, it is imperative that you, as a counselor aide, be oriented to the nature of the human learning process, the school in which you assist and the nature of your job. It is expected that you will continue to develop your skill and understanding through participation in a continuous in-service training program.[4]

---

[3] Ibid.

[4] James W. Costar, "Training Programs for School Counselor Aides," Department of Counseling, Personnel Services and Educational Psychology, Michigan State University, East Lansing, Michigan, 1970.

On the job training may be the most important phase of your training as a counselor aide because as an aide you are judged by the skill you exhibit in performing your tasks. This skill is developed only in the actual performance of the tasks, with constant close supervision a major factor in fostering the learning of proper techniques.

What Specific Duties can a Physical Education Aide Perform?

The increased size of physical education classes has resulted in little more than supervised mass recreation hours rather than physical education for the school children. In many schools, physical education, hygiene, recreation and sportsmanship falls on the teachers. Teachers who are not prepared to lead a class in physical activity are likely to cover their eyes and pray for the end of the hour.

As a physical education aide you can give physical education teachers more time to teach by taking care of routine chores such as attendance, giving written and skill tests, keeping records and charting progress, developing and preparing audio-visual aides, maintaining and dispersing equipment and policing locker rooms. In schools without specific physical education teachers, you can be insurance that the students are given some meaningful physical education.

As an aide you will often be able to take charge of a small group for instruction while the teacher works with the larger group or you may supervise the larger group while the teacher gives individualized instruction. You can also serve as a demonstrator or safety spotter when the class is using equipment that needs added supervision such as a trampoline.

If you are particularly skillfull in one area and are able to teach skills to the class which the teacher cannot, you can add to the range of classroom exposure for the students. It is possible that you may be an area specialist such as a first aid instructor or a nutritionist who can give the students more complete instruction than the classroom teacher could.

If you are a first aide instructor, trained and certified by the American Red Cross, you can give students knowledge that can save many lives.

The Red Cross also trains and certifies Water Safety Instructors. If you are a certified W.S.I., you could teach swimming and in so doing insure the students safety in water activities in and out of school.

In Covina Valley, California, where physical education teachers are available, an attempt is made to schedule at least one aide to each physical education teacher for each class period.[5] To give continuity to the program and develop sound teacher-teacher aide relationships, aides are requested to work at least two consecutive class hours.

Many of the Covina aides are college students and are not able to work a full school day, so the schools are likely to have two or three aides per day. In this way the college students are getting practical classroom experience and the schools are being staffed more adequately. For this project aides were initially sought in the college athletic departments and student placement bureaus, with special emphasis on potential physical education teachers.

For employment in this aide category, you should have had some training in physical education-type activities and have had experience in handling large groups.

---

[5] *How Aides Can Improve a Physical Education Program*, School Management, January, 1957, p. 57-8.

What Specific Duties can a Library Aide Perform?

As a library aide you will perform technical tasks of a non-professional nature under the direction of a professional librarian or other supervisor. Your tasks could include assisting students in gathering materials for reports, doing library research for the teachers, keeping library cards and records in order, helping to develop supplementary book and magazine lists and helping the librarian select books for the library.

As a library aide you would not perform tasks which require a professional knowledge of librarianship, but you would do such tasks as clerical functions. You could also perform technical tasks such as paging and circulating books, filing and typing, preparation and upkeep of library materials, maintenance of shelves, files and equipment, record keeping, cataloging and minor informational services such as answering directional questions about the use of basic reference tools.

You may receive your training in a terminal program offered by a local community college or in an in-service training program handled by the supervising librarian.

The college curriculum usually includes general education courses, library technical courses and related business and office courses.[6] General education courses would include communication skills, English composition, social sciences, humanities and physical sciences.

Library technical courses would include an introduction to libraries and library operation, circulation and information, media production and equipment handling and practical experience and supervised field work.

---

[6] *Draft of Guidelines for Training Programs for Library Technical Assistants,* Library Education Division, American Library Association, 50 E. Huron Street, Chicago, Illinois, April, 1968.

Business and office skills would include typing, business math, office machines, data processing, office management and operation of equipment and tools used in preparation and circulation of library materials.

In-service training by your supervising librarian would not include the general education courses but would include library technical skills and business and office skills as required by the needs of the particular library in which you will be employed.

Basic in-service training should include instruction in the Dewey Decimal System of shelving books and the location of various types of reference materials. The aide should also be trained to set-up and maintain a charge tray for materials circulated, store magazines, use the card catalogue and Reader's Guide to Periodicals and inventory library materials and set-up an attractive library resources display.

GLOSSARY

This glossary contains the author's interpretation of terms as applied to this text.

ACADEMIC	conforming to formalized scholastic functions, traditions and rules
ACADEMIC FREEDOM	that freedom which is granted to educators to teach their personal convictions and also that freedom allowing students to learn, inquire, or challenge in any field of exploration without fear of obstruction, dismissal, harassment or other reprisal
ACT-OUT	direct observable expression of feelings, usually hostile or aggressive feelings aimed at supervision or authority
ACT-UP	direct, observable expression of hostile or otherwise undesirable behavior
ADMINISTRATION	the physical process of attending to the function and operation of an institution
ADMINISTRATORS	those who are responsible for the structure and function of the school and its programs
ADULT OUT-REACH PROGRAM	school-related programs which are designed to bring the adult into the school community
ANCILLARY	referring to subordinate personnel employed to assist the professional with non-instructional duties
ANIMOSITY	expressed feelings of resentment or hostility
ARBITRARILY ASSIGNED	assignment of personnel made by the administrators with consideration of personality and ideological factors of personnel involved
AUDIO-VISUAL AIDS	material with sound and/or sight stimulus
AUXILIARY PERSONNEL	personnel employed to assist the professional in performing her duties
CAPACITY	limits of ability or responsibility
CATEGORICAL	in the form of a category
CATEGORY	division formed for the purpose of a given discussion or classification

CERTIFICATION	a statement by an official body which gives credibility to a person or institution which has met certain prescribed standards
CERTIFIED AIDE	an aide who has been certified by the state in which she is employed
CLASSIFICATION	grouping by similarities of subject, employment, etc., as systematic arrangement of job titles by responsibilities
CLASSLOAD	number of students in a classroom
CLASSROOM CHALLENGE	the task of meeting student needs
CLASSROOM ROUTINE	daily procedure developed in the individual classroom
COGNIZANT	awareness of the properties and relationships of an object
COMMENSURATE	equal to, corresponding in size, amount, degree of nature
COMMUNICATION GAP	the difference between what one person says and how another interprets it
COMMUNITY	a group of people living in the same locality or a given area unified by a common bond
COMMUNITY MORES	fixed local customs which have the force of law
COMPULSORY OBLIGATION	responsibility that must be fulfilled or the person responsible will be faced with reprimand
CONDUCIVE	helpful, contributive, encouraging environment
CONFIDENTIAL	private, not for general knowledge
CONSEQUENTIAL INFORMATION	information logically related so that the former validates the latter
CONTEMPORARY	at this time, current practice
CONTRIBUTION	the giving of ideas, assistance and/or moral support
CREATIVITY	ability to produce a work of thought or imagination, particularly art
CRITERIA	a test by which anything is evaluated in forming a pure and correct judgment respecting it

118

CRITERION	an evaluative standard on which a decision or judgment may be based
CULTURAL	pertaining to the knowledge, belief, art, morals, or customs and habits acquired by man as a member of his society
DEFICIENCIES	lack of normal development in intelligence or a lack of specified curriculum in the classroom
DEPLOYMENT	means of implementing employment for a specific task assignment
DIAGNOSTICIAN	one trained in identifying deficiencies from symptoms presented
DIFFERENTIATED ROLES	distinguishing behavior which is proper for each specific role
DIMENSION	scope or importance
DISCIPLINE	the inhibition of behavior
ECONOMIC FACTORS	sociological term describing the effect of income on environment
EDUCATIONAL PROCESS	the act of changing behavior, teaching students the desired information
EDUCATIONAL PURIST	one who believes in the traditional views of education
EFFICIENT	employment of the most acceptable means for the most productive ends
EMPLOYMENT	serving in a particular capacity with the purpose of financial gain
ENRICHMENT	to improve or to make more meaningful the means and matter of instruction
ENTITY	a distinct unit
ENVIRONMENT	external conditions and influences which affect the life and development of an organism
ENVIRONMENTAL CONDITIONING	knowledge acquired within the environment for acting in accordance with the behavior standards within the environment
EXEMPLARY	serving as an illustration or guide, generally that which is considered to be of the best

119

FEASIBILITY	practicality, capability of being completed successfully
FLOATER	an aide who moves from class to class and school to school as needed
FRINGE BENEFITS	benefits generally considered other than monetary, not of primary concern
GRADED SYSTEM	school systems using a class or grade-line division normally representing the work of one academic year, this term can be applied to either the students or to the tasks appropriate to a given year, a means of denoting student placement standing in the kindergarten through grade 12
IMPLEMENT	activate, put into effect
INCONSEQUENTIAL INFORMATION	information which is not meaningful to the particular subject
INCUMBENT	an obligatory act, imposed as a duty, responsibility or obligation
INDIGENOUS	quality gained from having lived in an area or community for an extended period of time
INDIGENT	in need of financial assistance
INDIVIDUALIZED INSTRUCTION	instruction designed to meet the needs of each individual student
INDOCTRINATE	to instruct in the rudiments or principles
INDUCEMENT	a persuasive element enticing one to behave in a particular manner
INGENUITY	inventiveness, cleverness, creativity
INHERENT	a permanent and unchangeable form existing in a person or object
INITIAL OUTLAY	the first expenditure of money or effort
INITIATE	to begin or start, to facilitate the first action
INITIATIVE	quality of drive and enthusiasm for beginning and carrying through projects
INNOVATIVE	a quality of being creative
INNOVATION	a new idea or practice

INNOVATORS	those who initiate new ideas and practices
INSTRUCTIONAL	giving new knowledge and direction
INTERNSHIP	period during which a student teacher would teach under the direct supervision of a certified teacher
JUSTIFICATION	the process of proving need or desirability of an act
LEGAL SANCTION	authority and credence given by law
MATRIARCHAL DOMINATION	overbundance of female authority
MATRICULATE	become a regularly enrolled member of the student body
MEDIATOR	one who acts to bring two conflicting persons together, usually by compromise
MONITOR	to watch an activity or operation and give warning when malfunction occurs
NEBULOUS	vague, without concrete grounds
NON-GRADED SYSTEM	a school system without the divisions which normally represent the work of the school year
NON-INSTRUCTIONAL	duties which are concerned with essential but non-teaching qualities
NON-PROFESSIONAL	duties which are not instructional or administrative
NON-TEACHING DUTIES	auxiliary, supportive duties
ORDERED	concrete structure with specific procedures
ORIENTATION	period during which you become accustomed to a new situation
PATRIARCHAL DOMINATION	situation in which the male is the authority figure
PERFUNCTORY OBLIGATIONS	routine duties
PHILOSOPHIES	a way of looking at and acting about an idea
PLACEMENT	arrangement or assignment
POTENTIAL	degree of ability not yet utilized

PREVENTIVE EDUCATIONAL MEASURES — measures aimed at preventing rather than remedying educational errors

PRIMARY AIM — the goal with which you are most concerned attaining

PROFESSIONAL — concerned with instructional or administrative duties

PROFESSIONAL DISTANCE — not becoming attached to or assimilated into a work or peer group below your professional status

PROFICIENT — able to do a job well

PSYCHOLOGICAL SET — a person's psychological make-up which causes him to act or react in a certain manner

PURISTS — those opposed to the introduction of new procedures and practices

RAMIFICATIONS — adverse reactions to an action

RAPPORT — a relationship in which there is understanding and free communication and expression

RATIONALIZATION — process by which one justifies actions, an ego-defensive method

REALISTICALLY — giving truths factually

REMEDIAL EDUCATION — education directed toward the student with limited abilities

SAMPLING — a representative group of the whole

SCAPEGOAT — person used for the displacement of guilt or aggression

SCHOOL POLICY — procedure for handling situations usually not deviated from

SCHOOL PROCEDURE — method of channeling information, requests and instruction

SECONDARY AIM — the second most important goal

SESSIONS — periods of time, usually relating to specific subjects such as orientation sessions

SIBLING — brothers and sisters of a particular child

SIGNIFICANT DIFFERENCE — credible element with substantial differential evidence

SIGNIFICANT FACTOR	an element which is credible and has substantial evidence
SIMULATION	a copy or act containing similarities but not the real thing
SOCIAL ENVIRONMENT	the surroundings, especially people, in which a person lives
SPORADICALLY SPACED	placed at random, not specifically or visibly ordered
STATUTES	a law declared by the legislature
STEREOTYPING	classing all people in one group and thereby giving them all the qualities of the group because they have one quality of that group
STIMULI	plural of "stimulus"
STIMULUS	a motivating or energizing factor
STRUCTURED	given shape, order and form
STUDENT IN-REACH PROGRAM	program designed to encourage and assist students in school
SUPERFICIAL	irrelevant and immaterial, not meaningful
SUPERVISING TEACHER	the professional teacher in charge of the classroom
TEACHER-TEACHER AIDE TEAM	cooperative work structure of a professional and a non-professional auxiliary
TEACHER TURNOVER	rate at which teachers leave a school system and must be replaced
TEACHING DUTIES	instructional tasks for which the teacher is responsible
TECHNOLOGY	applied science
TERMINOLOGY	choice and use of words
THEORETICAL	practice or belief supported by theory
THEORY	a general principle supported by considerable data
TRIVIA	insignificant material
TUTOR	the person in charge of the tutorial conference

TUTORIAL CONFERENCE

act of giving assistance to an individual or a small group

VINDICATE

free from any question of guilt or negligence

BIBLIOGRAPHY

Alexander, S. Kern, "What Teacher Aides Can-And Cannot—Do," *Nation's Schools*, Vol. 82, No. 2, August, 1968.

Bowman, Garda W., and Klopf, Gordon J., "New Careers and Roles in the American School." A study conducted for the Office of Economic Opportunity, New York: Bank Street College of Education, September, 1967, p. 36-37, p. 153-154.

Costar, James W., "Training Programs for School Counselor Aides," Department of Counseling, Personnel Services and Educational Psychology, Michigan State University, East Lansing, Michigan, 1970.

Edelfelt, Roy A., "The Teacher And His Staff," Virginia Journal of Education, April, 1967, p. 11-12.

Esbensen, Thorwald, "Should Teacher Aides Be More Than Clerks?" *Phi Delta Kappan* 47: 237: January, 1966.

Lacny, Clarence, Utilizing Teacher Aides in the Jackson, Michigan, Public Schools, "A Dual Opportunity," Jackson Public Schools, 1970.

Rioux, William J., "At The Teacher's Right Hand," *American Education*, December 1965 - January, 1966, p. 5-6.

PUBLIC DOCUMENTS AND REPORTS

A *Cooperative Study for the Better Utilization of Teacher Competencies*, Final Evaluation Report, An Evaluation Report Prepared by an Outside Evaluating Committee, Central Michigan University, Mt. Pleasant, Michigan, 1958, p. 27.

A *Look at Teacher Aides and Their Training*, Metropolitan Educational Research Association, Michigan State University, East Lansing, Michigan, 1968.

Auxiliary School Personnel: Their Roles, Training and Institutionalization, based on a nationwide study conducted for the U.S. Office of Economic Opportunity, Bank Street College of Education, New York, October, 1966.

Draft of Guidelines for Training Programs for Library Technical Assistants, Library Education Division, American Library Association, 50 E. Huron Street, Chicago, Illinois, April, 1968.

Education Profession Act, P.L. 90-35 Sec. 520, Title V, Part B., Higher Education Act of 1965, amended.

Estimates of School Statistics, 1967-68, National Education Association Research Report.

Guidelines for Special Programs for Educationally Deprived Children, Department of Health, Education and Welfare, Office of Education, Draft, October 5, 1965, p. 20.

How Aides Can Improve a Physical Education Program, School Management, January, 1957, p. 57-58.

"How the Profession Feels About Teacher Aides," *Teacher Opinion Poll,* NEA Journal, Vol. 56, No. 8, November, 1967.

NEA Research Bulletin, Vol. 47, No. 2, May, 1969.

Support Personnel for the Counselor: Their Technical and Non-Technical Roles and Preparation, Personnel and Guidance Journal, April, 1967.

Survey of Public School Teacher Aides, State Education Department, University of the State of New York, Bureau of School and Cultural Research, Albany, The Departmental, April, 1966.

Teacher Aides in the Classroom, A Digest, A New England Study Prepared by the New England Educational Assessment Project, A Cooperative Regional Report of the Six New England States, Providence, Rhode Island, 1967, p. 8.

Teacher Aides in Large School Systems, Educational Research Service Circular, No. 2, 1967, Washington, D. C., The Association, April, 1967, NEA Stock No. 219-06234, p. 1-2.

To What Extent Can Teacher Aides Free The Teacher's Time To Teach? U.S. News and World Report, May 11, 1956.